OTHER TITLES BY
DR. GREGORY POPCAK

CHRISTIAN LIVING

Broken Gods: Hope, Healing, and the Seven Longings of the Human Heart
(Image Catholic Books, 2015)

*The Life God Wants You to Have: Discovering the Divine Plan When Human
Plans Fail* (The Crossroad Publishing Company, 2011)

God Help Me, These PEOPLE Are Driving Me Nuts! Making Peace with Difficult People (The Crossroad Publishing Company, 2010)

*God Help Me, This STRESS Is Driving Me Crazy! Finding Balance Through
God's Grace* (The Crossroad Publishing Company, 2010)

MARRIAGE

For Better … FOREVER! (Our Sunday Visitor, 2015)

*Just Married: The Catholic Guide to Surviving and Thriving in the First Five
Years of Marriage* (Ave Maria Press, 2013)

How to Heal Your Marriage and Nurture Lasting Love (Sophia Institute
Press, 2017)

Holy Sex! The Catholic Guide to Toe-Curling, Mind-blowing, Infallible Loving
(The Crossroad Publishing Company, 2008)

Praying for and with Your Spouse: The Way to Deeper Love (The Word
Among Us, 2018)

PARENTING

Parenting with Grace: The Catholic Parents' Guide to Raising (almost) Perfect Kids (Our Sunday Visitor, 2010)

Beyond the Birds and the Bees: Raising Whole and Holy Kids (Ascension Press, 2012)

Discovering God Together: The Catholic Guide to Raising Faithful Kids (Sophia Institute Press, 2015)

Then Comes Baby: The Catholic Guide to Surviving & Thriving in the First Three Years of Parenthood (Ave Maria Press, 2014)

The BeDADitudes: 8 Ways to Be an Awesome Dad (Ave Maria Press, 2017)

The Corporal Works of Mommy (and Daddy Too) (Our Sunday Visitor, 2016)

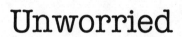

Unworried

Unworried

Unworried

A Life
Without
Anxiety

Dr. Gregory Popcak

**Our
Sunday
Visitor**
www.osv.com
Our Sunday Visitor Publishing Division
Our Sunday Visitor, Inc.
Huntington, Indiana 46750

Our Sunday Visitor Publishing Division
Our Sunday Visitor, Inc.
200 Noll Plaza
Huntington, IN 46750
1-800-348-2440

ISBN: 978-1-68192-169-3 (Inventory No. T1883)
eISBN: 978-1-68192-170-9
LCCN: 2018951826

Cover design: Tyler Ottinger
Cover art: Shutterstock
Interior design: Amanda Falk
Interior art: Jacob Popcak. Used by permission of the artist. All rights reserved.

PRINTED IN THE UNITED STATES OF AMERICA

CONTENTS

CHAPTER ONE

Have No Anxiety ... *At All!*

*Have no anxiety at all, but in everything, by prayer and petition, with
thanksgiving, make your requests known to God. Then the peace of God that
surpasses all understanding will guard your hearts and minds in Christ Jesus.*
(Philippians 4:6–7)

Have no anxiety … *at all?* Yes, Saint Paul said it. But did he *really* mean
it? He was just writing for effect, wasn't he? Or maybe it was possible to
live anxiety-free *back then*, when things were simple, and the only thing
people had to worry about was, well, martyrdom and stuff. But surely,
in our extremely busy, hyperlinked, post-modern, post-Christian, post-
truth society, we have a right to be at least a little terrified? Surely, we
moderns have more reasons than Saint Paul could have ever imagined to
find ourselves lying awake in a cold sweat at four in the morning while
our hearts beat out of our chest. Saint Paul couldn't have been talking
about us, right?

In fact, he was. He was speaking to all those who longed to follow
Christ, both in his time and for ages to come. As the Second Vatican
Council's Dogmatic Constitution on Divine Revelation, *Dei Verbum*,
says, "Sacred Scripture of both the Old and New Testaments are like a
mirror in which the pilgrim Church on earth looks at God, from whom
she has received everything, until she is brought finally to see Him as
He is, face to face (see 1 John 3:2)" (#7). Christians believe that God's
word is true for all times. We know our identity, our purpose, and our
path, not by what we *feel* is true in this moment, but in the truth of the
Word of God.

Saint Paul, both in his writings and in the example of his life and
death, lived what he taught, enduring hardship, imprisonment, unjust perse-
cution, and eventually death, not with terror, but with peace and grace. Paul,
however, certainly didn't invent this concept. Jesus constantly reminded his
followers, "Do not let your hearts be troubled" (Jn 14:1) and "do not worry"
(Mt 6:34). In John 14:27, Jesus says, "Peace I leave with you; my peace I give
to you. Not as the world gives do I give it to you. Do not let your hearts be
troubled or afraid." In Mark 5:36, Jesus says, "Do not be afraid; just have
faith."

Throughout both the Old and New Testaments, the authors of holy Scripture offer us an ocean of spiritual encouragement:

> Be strong and steadfast; have no fear or dread of them, for the LORD, your God, who marches with you; he will never fail you or forsake you. (Deuteronomy 31:6)

> Say to the fearful of heart:
>   Be strong, do not fear!
> Here is your God,
>   he comes with vindication;
> With divine recompense
>   he comes to save you. (Isaiah 35:4)

> Do not fear: I am with you;
>   do not be anxious: I am your God.
> I will strengthen you, I will help you,
>   I will uphold you with my victorious right hand. (Isaiah 41:10)

> Even though I walk through the valley of the shadow of death,
>   I will fear no evil, for you are with me;
>   your rod and your staff comfort me. (Psalm 23:4)

> The LORD is my light and my salvation;
>   whom should I fear?
> The LORD is my life's refuge
>   of whom should I be afraid? (Psalm 27:1)

> Cast your care upon the LORD,
>   who will give you support.
> He will never allow
>   the righteous to stumble. (Psalm 55:23)

> The LORD is with me; I am not afraid;
>> what can mortals do against me?
> The LORD is with me as my helper. (Psalm 118:6–7)

> For God did not give us a spirit of cowardice but rather of power and love and self-control. (2 Timothy 1:7)

> There is no fear in love, but perfect love drives out fear because fear has to do with punishment, and so one who fears is not yet perfect in love. (1 John 4:18)

> Cast all your worries upon him because he cares for you. (1 Peter 5:7)

Throughout Scripture, again and again, we hear that we are to not be afraid, that we must surrender our anxieties and worries to Christ, trust in the Lord, and be confident in God's providence, his deliverance, his mercy, and his constant care. As theologian Hans Urs von Balthasar once observed, "When one surveys even from a distance how often and how openly Sacred Scripture speaks of fear and anxiety, an initial conclusion presents itself: the Word of God is not afraid of fear or anxiety." What a powerful observation. We may fear anxiety and all the pressures that contribute to it, but the Word of God eschews that fear and bids us to do the same. Franklin D. Roosevelt once famously said, "We have nothing to fear but fear itself." God, however, wants to help us overcome even this. Yet it can still be hard to square all these scriptural assertions with the "real world," where anxiety seems like most people's full-time job.

LIFE IN THE "REAL WORLD"

"God must think I'm a horrible person."

Alison, a 34-year-old lawyer and mother of three, was struggling with anxiety that was seriously affecting her work and home life.

"I don't get it. I'm so blessed. I have a great job. A good family. But I'm on edge all the time." Her anxiety, which seemed to come from nowhere, had been building for several months. The last straw came when what she thought was having a heart attack at the office was actually diagnosed as a panic attack after an embarrassing ambulance trip to the ER. "I can usually accomplish anything I put my mind to, but no matter what I can't seem to power through this."

Alison discussed her situation with her pastor, who suggested both counseling and meditative prayer. While she welcomed his suggestions, she struggled with bringing her anxiety to God. "Every time I pray; I just feel so guilty. God's been so good to me. What kind of a way is this to say 'thank you' for all the blessings I've been given? My pastor told me that my anxiety isn't a sin, but it just feels so wrong on every level. I just feel like I'm letting God down."

Even if you aren't among the 20 percent of Americans who, like Alison, experience clinical levels of anxiety and panic attacks, chances are you are no stranger to at least the more common examples of anxiety. A friend of mine describes her tendency to "go from zero to widow in sixty seconds" when her husband is late from work. Another friend describes how he struggles to fall asleep every night because he is so worried about the problems at his workplace. I know so many good parents who constantly question whether they are ruining their children. How many of us watch the news with a growing sense of dread? And on Monday mornings, I'll bet there isn't a single reader who hasn't at least occasionally woken up feeling crushed by the weight of the new week.

HOW BAD IS IT?

The truth is, anxiety is such a commonplace experience that we often feel like there is something wrong with us when we *aren't* feeling anxious. We wonder what new threat to our security or peace we are missing and concern ourselves with what "fresh hell" (as Dorothy Parker put it) is waiting just around the corner, or in the next email.

But how do you know whether you are experiencing normal, garden-variety stress and anxiety or whether you are struggling with something more serious? When does anxiety become a disorder?

To be honest, if you have been asking yourself this question, it's probably time to at least seek a professional evaluation. People often wait for years (some research suggests an average of six years) before getting appropriate, professional counseling help. By then, the problem has been allowed to grow into something that has had a serious impact on the person's life, career, and relationships. Anxiety disorders, even serious ones, are very responsive to treatment. The vast majority of people who seek counseling for anxiety experience significant relief. By getting appropriate, professional help early, even before you're sure you "really" need it, you increase the chances of a shorter course of treatment and a quicker and fuller recovery.

That said, there are a few unmistakable signs that anxiety could be becoming a particularly serious issue for you. The quiz at the end of this chapter can help you decide if you are experiencing "normal" levels of anxiety or if you should seek an evaluation of your anxiety by a professional counselor.

THE GOOD NEWS

Regardless of the level of anxiety you are experiencing, the good news is that with proper help, you can find ways to stop worrying and significantly increase your peace. Better still, as a Christian, you can be comforted by realizing that whatever worry or anxiety you are feeling in this moment, it was never God's will that you be anxious. Neither are you destined to live in your anxiety.

In his *Theology of the Body*, Pope Saint John Paul the Great reminded us that to really understand God's plan for our life and relationships, we need to go back to the beginning. Saint John Paul proposed that there are three phases of human existence in the Divine Plan. *Original Man* is the first phase of human life before the Fall, when our first parents were still in total communion with God and each other and before God's plan was disrupted by sin. *Historical Man* is the post-Fall, sinful age we are living in now. *Eschatological Man* refers to our destiny at the end of time, when God creates the New Heaven and the New Earth and we are raised up in glory to become everything we were created to be and live in complete union with him for all of eternity.

"Great, Greg," you say. "What does any of this have to do with anxiety?" I'm glad you asked.

To figure out how things are supposed to be, and understand what God really intends for us, Saint John Paul II argued that it wasn't enough to see how things are now. We have to look at both God's intentions for us at the beginning of creation and what he intends us to become through his grace at the end of time. Too often, we are tempted to think that "what we see is what we get." It is too easy to believe that the anxiety-choked world we live in is all there is, and any thoughts about what we could become beyond the boundaries of our present reality are just wishful thinking. But the historical phase we live in cannot accurately reflect God's intentions for how we should live or relate or feel, any more than a defaced painting can represent the original intentions of the artist. Certainly, we can glimpse all the beauty that painting was meant to reflect, but only if we imagine what it looked like when it was first painted, or what it could look like again if it were to be restored.

Looking at the human condition from this perspective, we see that anxiety didn't enter the scene until sin entered the world. Prior to the Fall, God, man, woman, and creation lived in harmonious union. Genesis paints a picture of Adam and Eve confident in God's providence, safe in each other's arms, and happy to do the productive work of tending the garden. It was, literally, paradise.

After the Fall, everything shifts. Suddenly, man and woman, separated from God for the first time, are intimately aware of how alone, how vulnerable, how tiny they are, especially in the face of the enormity of the universe. They are naked and ashamed of just how incomplete, insufficient, and incapable they are of handling *anything* about the events their actions have set in motion. When they hear God coming, Adam and Eve have what amounts to the first panic attack. They hide in the bushes, cowering, feeling the weight of the wreckage closing in on them and hoping against hope that it would all just ... go away.

But God assures Adam and Eve, and us, that he did not intend to leave us this way. The Word would become flesh in the person of Christ, entering into the experience of historical man to tell us again and again to "be not afraid." He reminds us that when the new heavens and new earth are created at the end of time all will be set to right and peace will reign in the world and in our hearts once again.

> I heard a loud voice from the throne saying, "Behold, God's dwelling is with the human race. He will dwell with them and they will be his people and God himself will always be with them [as their God]. He will wipe every tear from their eyes, and there shall be no more death or mourning, wailing or pain, [for] the old order has passed away." (Rev 21:3–4).

Through all this we see that although anxiety is common enough in this present, historical phase of human existence, it is not God's intention either for our beginning or our end. The even better news is that we don't have to wait until the end times to be delivered from most if not all of our anxieties! God is already hard at work, healing us day by day by drawing us deeper and deeper into relationship with him, where we can encounter the perfect love that casts out all fear (cf. 1 Jn 4:18).

THE "MYSTERY" OF ANXIETY

To illustrate how God is working in our present lives to free us from anxiety, let's briefly turn to what we know about anxiety and spiritual development. Classic mystical theology teaches that there are three stages that each person moves through, by God's grace, on his or her road to sainthood: the Purgative Way, the Illuminative Way, and the Unitive Way. Most of us could count ourselves truly blessed to make it to the end of the first stage in our lifetime, the Purgative Way, where we learn self-mastery and surrender our attachment to neurotic comforts. Some may make it to the second stage, the Illuminative Way, where the soul experiences both the practical wisdom that comes from living a well-integrated life and a special sense of zeal for proclaiming the gospel not just with our words but also in the way we live and relate to others. A small few will be graced in their lifetime to achieve the third stage, the Unitive Way, where one experiences the beginnings of total union with God this side of heaven. The Unitive Way is the realm of living saints.

In his book, *Spiritual Passages*, the late psychologist and spiritual director Father Benedict Groeschel studied people he encountered along each of these three stages of the spiritual walk. He observed a steady decrease in anxiety and an increase in peace and trust in God's loving care, despite the trials a person encounters while moving through these stages and toward deeper communion with God.

This makes sense from both a psychological and spiritual standpoint. As we experience the integration that comes with self-mastery, the peace that accompanies finding healthy and godly ways to satisfy our deepest longings, the wisdom that helps us confidently discern the right thing to do at the right time and in the right way, and the all-encompassing love that comes from entering more and more deeply into the intimate presence of God, it stands to reason that anxiety would have less claim over our lives. We may have to wait until the next life for complete and total deliverance from anxiety. But it is God's will to allow us to experience however much peace we can — the peace the world cannot give (cf. Jn 14:27) — even while we are still in this world.

ARE YOU SAYING IT'S MY FAULT?

Upon learning that it was never God's intention that we would be anxious and that a decrease in anxiety usually can be expected to accompany greater spiritual maturity, many people can be left feeling that they are somehow to blame; that if they just worked or prayed harder, or somehow cared less about worldly things, maybe they could leave their worries behind. It can be easy to believe that having feelings of anxiety is somehow letting God down, or even sinful. People who are given to a type of anxiety known as scrupulosity are especially prone to this kind of thinking. The good news is that our anxiety cannot, does not, and could not ever let God down. No feeling — especially anxiety — can ever be sinful.

To commit a sin, we have to consciously *choose* to do what we know is wrong. Our actions must be willful, conscious, and at least reasonably informed (cf. CCC 1860–62). An emotion is none of these. Emotions, like anxiety, begin as pre-conscious, embodied experiences that bubble up, unbidden, from the limbic system (our emotional/reptilian brain) several milliseconds before our conscious mind is even aware of them. Emotions, including anxiety, can never be sinful because sin requires us to make a choice. Even though we can learn to change what we feel and how we act once an emotion appears on the scene, we can never choose what we feel in the first place. Anxiety, in particular, is a physiological and psychological response to the perception that, for some reason, we are not safe; that our physical, psychological, relational, or spiritual wellbeing is in jeopardy. Anxiety is meant to be a sign that we are facing imminent danger and that we should prepare to fight off the threat, flee from it, or freeze and hope it will just go away. Sometimes the reasons we feel threatened are obvious. Sometimes they are not. We'll look closer at this threat-basis for anxiety and where it comes from in a later chapter. But for now, you can see that the simple fact that a person feels unsafe — even extremely unsafe (and for not especially obvious reasons) — could not possibly be considered sinful. Anxiety is the perfectly predictable response to life in a fallen world where things truly are so often unsafe. More importantly, anxiety is an opportunity to experience the mercy and loving-kindness of a God who understands, better than we, how cruel this fallen world can be.

"MY GRACE IS SUFFICIENT"

But beyond knowing that anxiety is not sinful, it is encouraging to note that God doesn't require us to achieve anxiety-free status as a prerequisite for sainthood. NYU professor-emeritus of psychology, Paul Vitz, once published a paper noting that Saint Thérèse of Lisieux (who is not only a saint but also was proclaimed a "Doctor of the Church" for the wisdom of her writings) struggled with a serious separation anxiety disorder and anxiety in her younger years as a result of her sainted mother's premature death. Likewise, both Saint Alphonsus Ligouri and Saint Ignatius of Loyola famously battled with scrupulosity, which today can be understood as a variety of Obsessive-Compulsive Disorder that makes people anxious about spiritual, rather than bacterial, contamination. We should take comfort in knowing that sainthood depends much more on God's infinite mercy than upon our ability to achieve psychological perfection on our own merits. When Saint Paul experienced anxiety about his own inability to overcome certain flaws (2 Cor 12:9), God reassured him that, "My grace is sufficient for you, for power is made perfect in weakness."

SO WHAT?

At this point of the conversation, my clients often say something like, "Well, that's great and all, but knowing this doesn't make me feel any less anxious. What difference does any of this make to me?"

It makes all the difference in the world! We have a tendency to identify with our "emotional problems" in a way that we don't identify with "physical problems." I put these two terms in quotes because research shows that emotional problems are also physical, and many physical maladies (like heart disease, high blood pressure, irritable bowel syndrome, and fibromyalgia) have strong emotional connections. Regardless, when we get a virus, we don't say, "I am flu." We say, "I have the flu." But when struggle with anxiety, especially if we deal with chronic anxiety disorders, we do often say, "I am anxious" or "I am high strung" or something similar. It becomes an identity statement. Like, "Hi, my name is Bob. I have blue eyes and brown hair, and I am an anxious wreck." Um … nice to meet you?

The problem is, when we identify with the anxiety we feel, we begin to think of it as a necessary part of who we are. We may not like it, but there it is. We think we can't do anything about it. It's just part of us, so we have no choice but to accept it. As clients regularly tell me, "It's just how God wired me."

But think of how ridiculous this is. Even the person with an illness they can't do anything about still thinks of his or her "true" self as healthy. We say this all the time. "I woke up feeling under the weather. I can't wait to feel like myself again."

With anxiety, we have a tendency to assume that this is who we are. But if God did not create you to be anxious, and if he plans to deliver you from all anxiety in the fullness of time, then you may have anxiety today, you may even struggle against it tomorrow, but you are not "an anxious person." You are not defined by your anxiety, but by God's grace and the mighty work he longs to do in you. One day — whether in this life or the next — God intends to strip away your anxiety, and you will be free to be the peaceful person God created you to be. This is more than antics with semantics. It is a verbal recognition that you are meant for more; that the anxiety you feel is not a God-intended part of your make-up. With your good effort and God's grace, the odds are very good that you can make significant progress in lessening your anxiety (or even overcome it altogether) and feel like your "true" self again.

WHOLE, HEALED, GODLY, GRACE-FILLED

I like to ask my clients to imagine what I like to call their whole, healed, godly, grace-filled self (WHGG). This is not the super-hero self that doesn't have any problems. Rather, it is the ideal self that responds well to the various problems of life. Imagine, for a moment, a peaceful, confident, secure, strong, grace-filled you, who can face the various challenges you experience in your life with real courage, wisdom, and aplomb. It might seem like a fantasy, but humor me for a moment and imagine this person, who contends with the same things you manage, but does it with real grace, certainty, and peace.

Now here's the really shocking news: your WHGG self is not a fantasy. In fact, it represents *who you truly are.* When God looks at you, your whole, healed, godly, grace-filled self is who he sees, and who he is working to help you to become.

This may seem like utter nonsense the first time you consider it. Many of my anxious clients feel this way, but if you have children (or even know a child that you love), you might be able to naturally understand my point. Even if your child is having a bad day and making lots of mistakes, no loving parent would write their child off as a screw-up. You may see that your child is struggling, but you know who they really are. You know the good, strong, confident, talented person they are — even if they can't see it themselves or aren't currently behaving accordingly — and you dedicate yourself to helping them live up to all you see in them, all they can be. You want to help them discover that strength and lean into it so that they can exhibit those qualities consistently and confidently.

The same thing is true of the WHGG self. If you are feeling anxious, you might not feel like you are a strong, confident, courageous, secure, faithful, person today, but your heavenly Father sees through all that. He knows who you are underneath it all, and he has dedicated all of his grace to helping you become that. That doesn't mean you have to go from being an anxious wreck to being something else. It means that you already have the capacity to be a peaceful, strong, confident person dwelling within you in the seed God planted while you were still in your mother's womb.

Theologian Paul Tillich argues that God is the "ground of our being." In a sense, everything we are meant to be already *exists in God.* As we draw closer to God, all the stuff that isn't authentically part of us gets stripped away, and his grace allows us to become more ourselves. Grace does not take something that is horrible and turn it into something else. Grace peels away all the false layers our fallen world applies to us so that we can become more of who we truly are.

If you struggle with anxiety to any degree, I want you to understand that God is not asking you to become something that you are not. He simply wants you to learn how to nourish the seeds of peace, confidence, courage, strength, security, and all the rest that he has already planted in your heart so that those seeds, once germinated, can help you become the whole, healed, godly, grace-filled self that is already present in you but not yet fulfilled.

God literally created you with the physiological, psychological, and spiritual capacity to be the peaceful person you long to be. You just have to learn how to lean into that vision of yourself to "become what you are" (as Saint John Paul II was fond of saying). God has great plans for you. He wants to free you from your fears and deliver you from your anxieties so that you can rest confidently in his love and care like a child rests in its mother's arms. That was his intention for you from the beginning, and it is your destiny to be fulfilled through his grace. The first step is learning to stop clinging to our anxiety as if it was a necessary part of us, and cling, instead, to the perfect love of God, which will cast out all our fears.

That said, anxiety is a multifaceted problem with physical, psychological, emotional, relational, and spiritual factors contributing to it. Because these different factors come together in different ways in each person, everyone's anxiety profile is a little different. Over the next few chapters, I'll help you create a battle plan by enabling you to discover how, and to what degree, each of these factors may be contributing to your experience of anxiety. After that, we'll look at what you can do to help your body, mind, relationships, and faith start working for your good and strengthening your peace of mind. As we go along, I'll offer you several exercises that will help you apply the various concepts in each chapter to the specific circumstances of your life. To get the most benefit out of these exercises, I recommend grabbing a notebook and a pen and keeping them with you while you read so that you can complete them as you go.

Anxiety Quiz: How Bad Is It?

Answer True (T) or False (F) to the following.

_____ 1. Feelings of anxiety are making it difficult to fulfill my professional or personal obligations.

_____ 2. My anxiety causes me to feel uncomfortable around people or actively avoid opportunities to get together with others.

_____ 3. I have been forced to make changes in my life, work, or relationships to accommodate my anxiety.

_____ 4. When I feel anxious, I can't calm down unless I seek out repeated assurances from others.

_____ 5. My anxiety is making me irritable (whether you notice this or others tell you).

_____ 6. Worry and anxiety cause me to lie awake for at least some period most nights.

_____ 7. I constantly replay social interactions looking for mistakes I may have made or offenses I may have committed.

_____ 8. My doctor says I am healthy, but I experience consistent physical problems with (1 point for each).

___ fatigue	___ bowel	___ dizziness
___ muscle aches	problems	___ shortness
	___ sweating	of breath

_____ 9. I have experienced any of the above for the last six months or more (2 points).

Scoring
Unless otherwise directed (e.g., #8, #9), give yourself 1 point for each T answer.

Explanation of Results
Please note that this is not meant to be used as a tool to diagnose a specific type of anxiety disorder. There are many different anxiety disorders, and only a professional can help you properly identify the exact nature of the problem you are experiencing.

That said, because each of the above questions points to a symptom potentially associated with a serious problem with anxiety, *if you have 2 or more points*, you should speak to a professional counselor to discuss possible treatment options. Remember, anxiety is highly treatable. The quicker you get appropriate help, the sooner you can experience full recovery and start leading a more peaceful, confident, enjoyable life. If you are unaware of faithful, professional counseling resources in your area, contact the Pastoral Solutions Institute for assistance at CatholicCounselors.com or 740-266-6461.

CHAPTER TWO

The Anxious Brain

Anxiety is sneaky. It wears many masks. The more intensely a person experiences anxiety, the more difficult it can sometimes be for them to tell the difference between anxiety and a host of heightened emotional states such as excitement, anticipation, surprise, stress, nervousness, agitation, anger, frustration, and others. This confusion can be especially strong when a person is struggling with panic attacks. In such cases, something as benign as simply feeling excited about an upcoming birthday celebration can sometimes trigger fear that another panic attack is just around the corner if they allow themselves to get "too overstimulated." Ironically, obsessively attempting to live a less stressful or stimulating life can become its own stressor, as the person feels both overwhelmed by the impossibility of the task and suffocated by the sense that their life just keeps getting smaller and smaller. Agoraphobia — where a person can become so fearful that they cannot leave their house — is a perfect, albeit extreme, example of this.

Even people who do not experience crippling levels of anxiety can be helped by learning how to distinguish between the various emotional states that are often confused with or can lead to anxiety.

For instance, a prominent public speaker I once worked with perceived an increased heart rate, slight sweatiness, and light-headedness before speaking engagements. These feelings caused her to imagine a cascading series of events that would undoubtedly go wrong and ruin her talk and, ultimately, her career. Over the course of several sessions, I was able to help her reinterpret these sensations and come to see them not as anxiety but rather as a kind of anticipatory excitement — a sign that her body was ramping up to help her put on a dynamic presentation. Reframing her experience as an adaptive response — rather than a threatening one — helped her see that her body was actually trying to help her do a good job. Understanding these sensations in a new light enabled her to more effectively focus her mind on the performance she was about to give. Because excitement (along with most heightened emotional states) triggers increased heart rate and respiration, muscle tension, retinal dilation, and increased body temperature, including perspiration, excitement can easily be interpreted by the body as anxiety. This simple reframing intervention did not completely cure my client — who was struggling with other issues as well — but it did allow her to more effectively reinterpret and manage the physiological symptoms that were threatening her ability to go on stage.

AN OCEAN OF EMOTION

We'll talk more about how the mind creates your feelings (and can learn to change them) in the next chapter. For now, it's enough to know that every emotion begins with molecular shifts that occur throughout your body as you interact with the outside world. Neuroscientists refer to emotions as molecular action programs. Everything that happens to you, every choice you make, every thought you think, every response you make sends a wash of hormones, neurotransmitters, and other chemicals through your body. An emotion, then, is simply the process of your primitive brain (your limbic system) collecting all this information to allow you to identify the change that has occurred in your physical, psychological, relational, and/or spiritual well-being.

But that's a lot of information to gather. The primitive part of your brain responsible for collecting information about the molecular shifts in your body is too unsophisticated to say whether a particular change is good or bad, much less what you should do about it. That job belongs to a much more advanced part of your "thinking brain" called the insular cortex (IC). It's the IC's job to take all the information from the primitive brain about the various micro-shifts constantly occurring in your body and give that constellation of symptoms (heart rate, body temperature, degree of muscle tension, respiration, chemical shifts, etc.) a label that identifies it as a particular emotion. Having labeled it, the IC then sends messages back down to the primitive brain so it can tell your body how to adjust or what behaviors to enact so that you can function most effectively in any given situation.

I LOVE LUCY'S BRAIN

The IC usually does a great job, but when it gets bombarded with too much information too fast, sometimes the process breaks down. There is an old gag that first aired on the classic television program *I Love Lucy*. Lucy and her friend Ethel are at work in a chocolate factory. Their job is to wrap the chocolates that roll past them on a conveyor belt so that they are ready for packing. The supervisor, fed up with them for having failed at every other job in the plant, tells them that if even one chocolate goes to the packing department unwrapped, Lucy and Ethel will be fired.

It all starts out just fine. The chocolates roll past at a manageable pace, and Lucy and Ethel capably and confidently wrap each piece. Suddenly the conveyor belt starts speeding up. They have to move faster and faster. Pretty soon, they are mortified to discover that they just can't keep up. In desperation, Lucy and Ethel start shoving chocolates in their mouths, stuffing them down the front of their dresses, hiding them in their chef's hats, hiding them around the room — *anything* to prevent the chocolates from getting to the packing department unwrapped and costing them their jobs. The supervisor comes out and, failing to notice that their mouths and uniforms are bursting with candy, sees that the conveyor belt is empty, compliments them on their good work, and yells up the production line, "Speed it up a little!"

Sometimes, especially when people struggle with chronic anxiety, the IC is like Lucy in the chocolate factory. The primitive brain/limbic system is throwing so much information at it so quickly, the IC just can't wrap each emotion in the correct package. Eventually it gets overwhelmed, labels everything "anxiety" just to get it over with, and goes fishing.

Why does this happen? For some people it's because they have either lived through prolonged, traumatic events or at least experienced singularly stressful situations that left their nervous systems stressed and overwhelmed. For these folks, their IC gave up a long time ago. As a result, every time they experience almost any heightened emotional state (excitement, stress, anger, anticipation), it feels like anxiety.

Other people may not have experienced particularly traumatic events in life, but they simply have an underdeveloped IC that can't process information as rapidly as it should. The good news is that, for either of the above groups, brain research shows that the brain is like a muscle. Just like physical exercise builds muscle tissue, creating bigger muscles, different thinking exercises and behaviors create thicker, faster neural connections between different parts of the brain. The process by which we can "beef up" the volume of different structures in the brain is called *neuroplasticity*. Neuroplasticity allows the brain to constantly rewire itself so that it can retain new information and adapt to new environments.

A BODY OF FEAR

The process of reframing that I described at the beginning of this chapter (in the story of my public speaker client) is one simple exercise that helps the IC learn (or, in some cases, relearn) its job of wrapping and packaging emotions correctly. Consciously renaming a particular experience as something else teaches the IC to stop automatically slapping an "anxiety" wrapper on every heightened state that bubbles up from the primitive brain and, instead, be more and more sophisticated and efficient at detecting subtle differences between different heightened states.

It is beyond the scope of this book to help you identify all the different feelings that can masquerade as anxiety or trigger feelings of anxiety. But the most important distinction to make is the one between anxiety and fear. Although people commonly use these two terms interchangeably, from a psychological perspective they are quite different. Fear is the natural, biological, and appropriate response to an imminent threat. Anxiety is when the brain's natural fear circuits get hijacked by something that isn't an immediate danger or could even be good for us (for instance, accepting a great new job or standing up for ourselves). In a sense, anxiety is fear's evil twin.

We develop the capacity for fear early. By eight months in utero, a baby's fear and protection circuitry is fully developed and ready for action. Throughout life, in the face of a real threat, this circuitry injects chemicals into our brain and bloodstream to ramp up our senses and speed up our reaction time so that we can see all the ways we could respond and, if necessary, escape. When the fear-systems in our brain work properly, they serve a protective function, warning us away from danger and easing off once the threat has passed.

Anxiety hijacks this God-given fear-threat system and causes us either to fear things that could be good for us (e.g., new opportunities, commitment in a healthy relationship), experience disproportionate responses (either in intensity or duration) to actual threats, or suffer feelings of panic when, in fact, no danger exists (e.g., panic attacks).

In short, fear, as unpleasant as it may be, can be a great gift, a servant of our physical, emotional, and spiritual health and well-being. But anxiety represents a threat to our physical, emotional, and spiritual integrity that, left unchecked, can tear our lives apart.

FEELING BURNED OUT?

People often say they feel "burned out" by their struggles with anxiety, but most are unaware of the deeper truth behind this metaphor. Imagine soaking your hands in bleach for several hours, even days. You would get a chemical burn that left your skin severely raw and irritated. Even brushing up against something afterward might hurt tremendously. In a similar way, the chemicals (glucocorticoids) produced by the brain's fear response are caustic. When persistently stressful or traumatic events trigger prolonged or too intense exposure to these chemicals, they create something like a chemical burn on your amygdala, the CEO of the fear/protection system. At the very least, this can cause us to feel every stressor more acutely, making it harder to respond in a calm, rational way. If anxiety persists, the amygdala blasts chemicals at another part of the brain called the hippocampus, which stores emotional memories.

If the amygdala is the CEO of your fear/protection system, the hippocampus is the board secretary. While the amygdala is triggered in the presence of a threat, it's the hippocampus' job to "take notes" and remember that a particular event was anxiety-producing in the past. The next time you encounter that same event, or even something remotely similar, the hippocampus triggers the amygdala and reminds you that you "should" feel anxious — even if there is no practical immediate threat present. In the face of long-term stress, or an unusually traumatic stressor, the amygdala can blast so many stress chemicals at the hippocampus that it can cause it to shrink (like you might curl up in a ball if someone was yelling at you for a long time). When this happens, we tend to become less emotionally flexible and more easily stuck in unpleasant emotional states. In a sense, as the hippocampus shrinks, the secretary loses the notebooks filled with our happy memories and resourceful ideas and retains only the notebooks filled with frightening, scary, and traumatic experiences. Although this is not a pleasant experience, our brain responds this way to constant or overwhelming stress so that we can always be ready to respond to whatever new threats come our way.

At its best, this partnership between the amygdala and hippocampus enables us to anticipate and head off potential problems. At worst, it causes us to develop an anxiety disorder in which an undercurrent of constant worry or even bursts of terror intrude upon every aspect of our lives.

The takeaway from all this is that even though fear and anxiety feel very similar to one another — because they both are produced by the same fear-threat system in your brain — they are very different phenomena. The person experiencing fear reacts because they are having a genuinely protective, biologically pre-programmed reaction to an imminent threat to their safety or wellbeing. For instance, if you cross the street and notice a car bearing down on you, fear causes you to run across the street to get out of the car's way. If someone was chasing you, intending to do you harm, fear would cause you to run faster to try to get away. If you were unable to escape, fear would enable you to fight back and defend yourself against your attacker. In the worst case, if you couldn't get away, fear would cause you to try to hide and be as still as possible in the hopes of escaping your pursuer. As distressing as all these scenarios might be, they make sense. All these different responses to these various threats are adaptive. They are intended to preserve your life and safety. An immediate threat to your wellbeing provokes an immediate, defensive response.

Anxiety, on the other hand, is akin to suffering a pinched nerve in the brain's fear-threat system. The pain is real enough, but it's the result of something happening inside of you, *and not a response to an external, physical threat.* For instance, if you had a pinched nerve in your leg, you wouldn't call an ambulance. You would feel pain, and it might hurt terribly, but you would (1) recognize that the pain was coming from the inside of your body, not from an outside assault; (2) focus your attention on trying to breathe through the cramp and relax your leg; and (3) eventually engage in some limited exercise to work through any remaining soreness.

THREE STEPS TO ANXIETY FIRST-AID

One of the simplest ways to help your brain do a better job of dealing with anxiety is similar to that intuitive three-step approach I described that most people use for dealing with any other pinched nerve in their body: Relabel, Reattribute, and Respond. These steps are adapted from psychologist Jeffrey Schwartz's groundbreaking work treating OCD as described in his book *Brain Lock*.

Step One: Relabel the Threat

You feel anxious. Don't act out. Don't start thinking obsessively about what you can or should do to try to get control of whatever is happening around you. Instead, check the feeling. Ask yourself, "Am I responding to an imminent (not a past or potential future) threat to my life or safety?"

Remember, fear is an appropriate response to an imminent threat. It kicks you into high gear in the moment so that you can escape some clear and present danger — and then it goes away. That's how fear is supposed to work.

Anxiety, on the other hand, tends to be a fear response triggered by something that has either happened a long time ago, has not yet happened, or may not actually be happening at all. Likewise, instead of kicking you into high gear so you can escape an imminent threat to your life or safety, anxiety tends to hang around and haunt you. For instance, if you are afraid you might have said something embarrassing while out to dinner with your friends last week, you might keep replaying the scene over and over in your head and experience a low-grade sense of dread. Or if you have to give a presentation at work next week, you might imagine all the ways you might make a fool of yourself and struggle with a constant feeling of dread and terror. Or, alternatively, for no reason at all, you might just be suddenly struck with an overwhelming sense of panic that causes you to feel like something terrible is going to happen.

The feelings associated with each of these experiences is not fear, but rather anxiety, because you are not responding to an imminent and obvious threat to your safety or wellbeing. In each of these instances, your fear-threat system — the part of your brain that is supposed to help you respond to imminent threats to your health and safety — is actually being hijacked by something that may be concerning but is certainly not an imminent threat.

What difference does this make? It means that in each of these cases, you are not really experiencing fear. Rather, you *feel* fearful in these instances because the concerning event caused a misfiring of your fear-threat system. This is a small, but significant difference. It means that the answer to your problem — despite how you might be feeling — is not obsessively thinking about how you could apologize for an offense you're not even sure you committed, staying up all night trying to figure out how you are going to pay your bills and where you are going to live after your boss fires you for messing up the presentation, or obsessively looking around for something — anything — to blame for your looming sense of panic and dread. Instead, you must step back and help your insular cortex relabel your experience of anxiety, *not as a reasonable reaction to an obviously threatening situation*, but rather as a sign that your fear circuits in your brain are misfiring. Instead of running around trying to figure out how you can fix something going on around you, you must instead figure out how to control your brain and body. Then, and only then, will you be able to correctly assess what to do about the situation itself.

Step Two: Reattribute (and Relax)

Once you have determined (however tentatively) that the situation triggering your anxiety is not the source of any imminent, immediate danger, the second step is to relax your body. As I indicated above, instead of continuing to tell yourself that "I am anxious because X (non-life-threatening event) happened" you must *reattribute* the anxiety you feel to a "pinched nerve" in your brain that results in the misfiring of your fear-threat system. You can then intentionally shift your focus away from the concerning event for the time being (we'll come back to it in a minute) and refocus on relaxing your body and getting your fear-threat system back under control.

I want to be clear. In stating this, I am not saying that your anxiety is not real. It is very real. Because anxiety hijacks the fear-threat system, you are feeling genuine fear, perhaps even a crushing amount. What you are reading here should not be interpreted to suggest that your anxiety isn't a serious problem. In fact, what I am asserting is that more than some figment of your imagination, problems with anxiety are always serious physiological events. The good news, however, is that rather than being made fearful because of some situation that is largely outside of your control, your anxiety is actually being caused by a process that, with practice, you can learn to control.

Anxiety is controlled by two different systems in the Autonomic Nervous System, the neurological system that is responsible for things like heart rate, respiration, blood vessel constriction, temperature, etc. The sympathetic nervous system (your "speed up" system) acts like a gas pedal. Stimulating it makes your bodily systems race. By contrast, the parasympathetic nervous system (your "slow-down" system) is like a brake pedal. These two systems function in harmony with one another, but they can also function independently — just like the gas and brake pedals on your car can be used separately or simultaneously depending on what the situation calls for.

When you feel anxious, your "speed up" (sympathetic) nervous system is being hyper-activated. In essence, the gas pedal is floored and stuck. The good news is that you can unstick the gas pedal by tapping the brake, i.e., activating the parasympathetic nervous system. At first, your metaphorical engine might continue racing, even after you've applied the break. But within about fifteen to twenty minutes, your brain should re-regulate and sync back up again. With practice, it's possible to learn to get this process to happen within seconds. There are actually a few simple ways to do this.

One of the most effective, yet simplest, techniques involves consciously speaking and acting more slowly than you feel like you want to. Often, when we are anxious, our thoughts and speech automatically race. On top of this, because our brain is preoccupied with being anxious, we stop paying attention to what we are doing. Both of these symptoms are signs that our sympathetic (speed-up) nervous system is over-engaged.

But we can learn to reach down and "unstick" the gas pedal by intentionally activating our parasympathetic nervous system (slow-down system). Intentionally speaking a little slower than we want to, acting a little more slowly and intentionally than we naturally prefer in that moment, and forcing ourselves to pay attention to what we are doing taps the brake pedal. This creates little bit of a jarring sensation as the speed-up and slow-down nervous systems try to sync up with each other. They don't like to be at odds with each other, so consciously depressing the brake on the slow-down nervous system unsticks the gas pedal and forces the speed-up nervous system to stop racing.

We'll discuss more sophisticated interventions later in the book, but here are a few other simple techniques that can help you consciously regain control of your runaway speed up nervous system.

Deep breathing exercises can be tremendously helpful for getting your sympathetic nervous system unstuck. Here is a simple one. Place one hand on your stomach and one hand on your chest. Close your eyes. Breathe in through your nose for the count of four, hold your breath for the count of seven, and blow out through your mouth to the count of eight. Repeat for at least five minutes or until the anxiety passes.

To someone struggling with anxiety, suggesting that they should breathe deeply can seem remarkably stupid and banal, but it turns out there is solid science behind it. Recent research by scientists at Stanford University School of Medicine found a small patch of 175 nerves, deep in the brainstem, that act as an emotional pacemaker. These nerves monitor how quickly you are breathing and relay that information to a different part of the brain that monitors your state of mind. It turns out that you can trick these nerves into thinking that you are calmer than you actually feel by intentionally breathing deeply and slowing down your respiration rate. Although you might be tempted to dismiss the power of simple suggestions like "take a deep breath" for relieving anxiety, science shows you may be missing out if you do.

Reflective prayer (as opposed to "*Help! God, save me!*") is also very helpful to "tap the brake" and slow down your brain and body. We'll discuss spiritual interventions for anxiety in more depth later, but a simple way to employ prayer is to close your eyes and intentionally recall the times God has been faithful to you or carried you through a difficult time. Take a moment to praise God for these things. Your heart won't be in it at first, but that's okay. It's what Saint Paul called a "sacrifice of praise" (Heb 13:15), and it helps to remind you of the fact that if God has been present to you so many different times in the past, he isn't going to fail you now. It also reminds you of all the other times you were sure your life was going to irreparably fall apart, but miraculously it didn't.

Grounding is another simple way to "tap the break" on your slow-down nervous system. Grounding reconnects you with your body and the present moment instead of letting you fly away with your thoughts. Count five things you see, four things you hear, three sensations you are feeling in your body. Identify two people who care about you, and one simple thing you could do to feel even a tiny bit better right now (for instance: have a hot cup of tea, listen to your favorite music, do something you enjoy for a few moments). This technique works because anxiety wants your thoughts to race ahead to anticipate all possible future problems. Forcing yourself to re-focus on the present moment, especially at this level of detail, activates your para-sympathetic nervous system and slows the anxious brain's tendency to race ahead.

Finally, **reconnecting** with others can be tremendously important. Go to your spouse or a good friend and ask them to give you a hug. Don't be quick about it. Relax into the hug until you feel yourself exhaling the stress. Hugging actually syncs your heart rate to the other person and increases the presence of oxytocin, a powerful "calm down" hormone produced through interpersonal bonding.

Each of these simple exercises, alone or together, have been shown to have a powerful impact on the autonomic nervous system, causing it to let up on the gas and depress the brake and at the same time rapidly decelerate the stress response.

The problem is, most people think doing any of these things is nonsense. "How is breathing and getting a hug going to stop me from losing my job when I screw up my presentation? Don't be an idiot!"

Remember, unless there is an immediate threat to your life or wellbeing, you should not be experiencing fear. If you are, something in your nervous system is misfiring. The more you ignore this simple biological fact and instead try to control all the outside factors that might be causing the anxiety, the more anxious and out of control you will feel. Because you are ignoring the real cause of your anxiety, the unnecessary or disproportionate triggering of your autonomic fear response, any attempts to "fix" the problem by trying to control your external world will simply backfire. First, remind yourself that having a legitimate concern about X does not mean that X is an imminent threat, and *then* refocus on getting this fear-threat system back under control. You will be able to consciously and intentionally restore a sense of peace and confidence.

At first, with any of these exercises, depending on the intensity of your experience and how long you have been suffering from anxiety, it might take up to fifteen to twenty minutes of concentrated effort to get yourself back under control. With consistent practice, however, you can reduce this time to mere seconds.

The point is, anxiety — unlike fear — is not a reaction to your environment. Anxiety may be triggered by context, but it is *caused* by a misfiring of the autonomic nervous system (the combined speed-up/slow-down nervous systems). Because of this, your best hope for reclaiming a sense of peace is to focus primarily on getting control of your body rather than your environment.

Step Three: Respond

The final step in the Relabel-Reattribute-Respond process is addressing the situation that triggered the misfiring of your fear-threat system. Again, just because your anxiety wasn't strictly caused by something outside of you doesn't mean there isn't a real problem to deal with. It's just to say that the particular stressor shouldn't be producing the kind of intense, fearful panic usually reserved for an imminent, physical threat.

Now that in step 2 you successfully reattributed your experience of anxiety as a misfiring of your fear-threat system and used several of the suggestions you read above to get your fear-threat system back under control, you're ready to do something productive about the situation that inadvertently triggered the misfiring of your fear-threat system.

When you are stuck in an anxious response, you can't effectively problem-solve. You can only react to a problem, which will probably cause you to do something impulsive that can only make things worse. But if you take the time to calm your body down, turn off your fear-based reactive brain, and turn on your thinking brain, you will be in a much better place to respond to the specific event that triggered your anxiety.

The key is "think small." In fact, the smaller the better. You might not be able to identify the "one big solution" to the problem of your unsupportive marriage, but you can place a call to a marriage therapist right now. You might not be able to figure out how to not prevent your antagonistic boss from firing you, but you can ask yourself how you could do your absolute best on the next step of the project you are working on and write down some ideas, or you could even get your resume together and start looking for a different position. If you can't think of even the smallest change you could make to affect the problem, then at least ask yourself how you could take a little better care of yourself. Perhaps you could take a walk, call a friend, pray, or do something you enjoy, even for a few minutes.

One of the chief antidotes to anxiety is thoughtful, productive action as opposed to the "chicken-with-your-head-cut-off" reaction that occurs before you have gotten your body under control. If you can convince yourself to make even a small change that helps you respond more effectively to the problem or improves your mood, you will feel more powerful. When you make yourself pursue even a tiny change, you'll be surprised at how little it actually takes to regain a sense of power in your life, and how much of an impact this sense of personal power has on helping you overcome anxiety.

This three-step process of **Relabel-Reattribute-Respond** is a simple but powerful way to begin to master those feelings of anxiety that threaten to master you. Begin practicing these tools today. Even if they don't take away all of the anxiety you feel, they will decrease your overall emotional temperature and help you use the more sophisticated anxiety-busting techniques we will discuss in future chapters. You will be taking some of the first, important steps down the road to a life without anxiety.

EXERCISE: Relabel, Reattribute, Respond

Directions: Use the following exercise for any situation that causes you anxiety.

1. **Relabel.**
   - ❑ Identify a situation that causes you anxiety. Write it in your notebook.

   - ❑ Does this situation represent an imminent threat (not a potential, future threat) to your health or safety? Yes or No?

     - ▪ If YES, your fear response is legitimate. Do what you must to escape the situation.
     - ▪ If NO, then you probably need to respond to this situation rather than react to it. Proceed to step 2.

2. **Reattribute.**
   - ❑ The situation itself may or may not be serious, but your emotional reaction is probably disproportionate. Your emotional reaction is caused not by the situation, but by the fact that the situation has hijacked your fear-threat system. DO NOT respond to the situation at this time. Focus on getting control of your body by doing any/all of the following.

     - ▪ **Intentionally slow your rate of speech.** Let you mind catch up with your mouth. Slow down until you have eliminated all "um's" and "ah's" and can speak what you are thinking calmly, thoughtfully, and without hesitation.
     - ▪ **Deliberately slow down your actions.** Focus on what you are doing. If your mind is racing ahead to the next activity, bring it back. No matter how mundane the current task is (i.e., reaching for a glass, walking through a room) focus your mind total-

ly on what you are doing in this moment.

- **Breathe.** Use the four-seven-eight breathing technique described in this chapter. Repeat for at least five minutes or until the anxiety decreases or passes.

- **Pray.** Concentrate on specific times you have felt God's love. Remember times when God delivered you from difficulties. Thank him for these times. Praise him for his constant love and providence. Ask him for the grace to believe that he is right here for you in this moment in the same way, loving you, providing for you, and delivering you just as he always has.

- **Make connection.** Is there someone who could give you a hug? Go to them. Don't talk about your problem ... yet. Just tell them you are feeling out of sorts and need some help pulling yourself together. Relax into the hug. Focus on matching their breathing. Sync your body to theirs. If possible, stay in the hug until you find yourself exhaling spontaneously. That lets you know your "calm down" nervous system is fully engaged.

3. **Respond.**

❑ Now that you have gotten your body and brain back under control, you are ready to respond (rather than react) to the situation that hijacked your fear system in the first place.

❑ What is one small step you can take to make the situation even a little bit better? Do not look for what you can do to resolve the whole situation once and for all. Just look for one small, even tiny, thing you can do right now to make a small improvement. Do that thing.

❑ Or, if nothing can or should be done at this time, look for one small thing you can do to help you refocus on making the rest of the day as pleasant as possible despite this troubling situation. Do that thing.

The goal of this exercise is to: 1. Help you identify the real source of your anxiety (your body, not your environment); 2. Re-engage your calm-down nervous system so you can respond rather than react to stressors; and 3. Identify one simple step you can take to effectively respond to the problem situation. This process will allow you to, one step at a time, take control of your anxiety and respond more thoughtfully and productively to life's stressors.

CHAPTER THREE

Getting on My Nerves — The Psychology of Anxiety

The more you understand the different factors that work together to create our experience of anxiety, the more avenues you have to address and overcome it. In the last chapter, we explored how anxiety begins as an experience inside your body, and we identified some basic strategies that can help you get your body back under control. Now we are going to briefly explore how your thought-life can also be a significant contributor to your level of anxiety and begin to look at different psychological strategies that can help anyone experience greater peace regardless of the level of anxiety they might be experiencing in their lives.

PSYCHOLOGICAL AND EMOTIONAL FACTORS

Although we often don't realize it, when something happens to us, it impacts us on several different psychological and emotional levels at once. Let's pick a simple illustration. Suppose you text a friend and you don't get a response. As a result, you begin to experience some degree of anxiety.

The First Layer — The Event

From a psychological perspective, the first layer of experience is the event itself. You texted a friend and didn't get a response. As a result, you are aware of a feeling of nervousness and dread. But why? Most people answer this question by simply describing what happened, as if that explains everything. "I just told you! I texted my friend and didn't get a response! How could I NOT feel anxious and upset?"

The problem is that this statement assumes that everyone would feel the exact same way about this event as you do. Although many people feel anxious when a friend doesn't text them back, some people feel angry, some people are curious, and others don't give it a second thought. Even among those who get anxious, they might be more or less anxious than you. The real question is, what is causing your unique emotional reaction?

The Second Layer — Self-Talk

To answer this question, you have to go a little deeper. The second layer of any emotional experience is *self-talk*. Self-talk is the internal narration of your life. We aren't always paying attention to it, but our mind is always engaging in some kind of self-talk as a way of telling us what our current experience means to us, what we should make of it, and how we should respond to it based on past experience. One good example of self-talk are those internet memes that show a person thinking two different thoughts: the thing they say to be polite and the thing that they really think.

> *Karen texted Julia an adorable cat video. Julia didn't respond.*
> *Karen smiled and said, "It's fine ..."*
> *It was NOT fine.*

To get at the particular self-talk that attends a specific emotional event, rather than asking, "Why do I feel this way?" which tends to simply lead to circular reasoning (i.e., "I feel this way about the event because the event happened!"), it's better to ask yourself, "What does it mean to me that this event happened?" Or even, "What does it say about me that this happened to me?" Both of these questions do a better job of helping us tune in to the self-talk that underlies our anxiety.

> "What does it mean to me that Julia didn't respond to my text?"
> *"It means that I've annoyed her and she's trying to distance herself from me!"*

> "What does it say about me that Julia didn't respond to my text?"
> *"Obviously, it means that I'm a pest who makes people uncomfortable and drives away everyone I care about."*

Granted, this is an extreme response, but it's a surprisingly common one. Maybe you have even felt this way from time to time. Of course, you might have a different response entirely. Another person might answer these questions in the following way.

> "What does it mean to me that Julia didn't respond to my text?"
>
> *"It means that she's busy and didn't have time to look at a cat video even though it was really adorable."*
>
> "What does it say about me that Julia didn't respond to my text?"
>
> *"It just says that I picked the wrong time to share this. No big deal, I'll just show her when we get together next time."*

Obviously, a person whose mind was engaging in this kind of self-talk would not experience much, if any, anxiety about Julia's lack of response. This is usually when my client says, "But how does Karen know she didn't drive Julia away? What if Julia does think she's annoying?"

Of course, the answer to this is that Karen has no idea at all what Julia is thinking. She could be thinking one of a million possible things, and "Boy, that Karen and her stupid cat videos really burn my toast" could be one of them. If that were the case, assuming that Karen took the time to ask Julia what was going on, she and Julia could work through it together and become better friends because of it. But how often do we actually stop to ask the other person what they are really thinking before we respond to them — or even react to them? Most of the time, in the absence of any other actual evidence, we assume our automatic interpretations of the event are correct. We allow our actions to be informed by these erroneous thoughts, often causing ourselves to feel powerless, isolated, self-pitying, and anxiety-ridden in the process. The situation is real, but our interpretation and reaction are entirely self-created. So, where do these interpretations come from? They come from the third layer of our psychological experience.

The Third Layer — Memories

When something happens to us, our right brain does a quick, gut-level search through our bank of life experiences to find the past experience that most resembles this present event. Our right brain has less than a second to sort through all our memories and choose one that best compares with the present experience so we have some idea of how to respond, even in the absence of additional information. Considering how much information it has to sort through in so little time, our right brain does a phenomenal job of correctly associating present experiences with past events to help us formulate appropriate, proportionate, and productive responses to what is going on in the here and now. But sometimes the process goes a little haywire. For instance, what if something your wife says makes your right brain recall some hurtful thing your mother said when you were five? In that case, it will make perfect sense to you that the only logical response is to pout — or even throw a tantrum. Of course, this response will seem completely insane to your wife, who would have no idea why you're acting that way.

Worse, what if your memory bank is filled with unhealthy experiences of people treating you poorly through neglect or abuse? These experiences are not uncommon, but fortunately, they don't define the way most human beings normally treat each other. Even so, if those are the only experiences your right brain has to choose from when it looks for a guide to current events, you'll automatically assume — on an unconscious, gut level — that many people have more malicious intent than they actually do. For instance, a study by the University of Vermont published in the *Journal of Social and Personal Relationships* showed that children raised in households where moms and dads engaged in non-abusive but chronic arguing were more likely to assume a negative intention behind even the neutral actions of others. Their brains were primed to assume the worst about others, because when they encountered a new social situation, their right brains took them back to memories of people assuming the worst about each other.

To understand where your particular brand of self-talk originates, it is helpful to ask the question, "What experiences taught me to feel that way?"

To answer this question, you're not looking for that time on Wednesday, September 4, when your mom sat you down and said, "Now, honey, when someone doesn't return a text right away, that means they hate you and you've driven them out of your life. Got that, dear?"

Resist the temptation to overthink this. Instead, sit with the feeling you are having and reflect on the thought going through your head. In our example, Karen's thought is, "I'm an annoying pest who drives away people I care about." As she reflects on this thought, she should allow whatever memories that may be associated with that thought to float up to the surface of her mind. These memories don't have to make sense. Often, our first reaction to these memories will be, "That couldn't have anything to do with this. Don't be silly." She should just sit with it, trust the process, and write down whatever memories come up, regardless of what they are.

As our fictional client, Karen, does this exercise, perhaps she will be reminded of a time when she was bullied in grade school, or a time when her sister refused to play with her and called her a "pest," or her father was having a bad day and carelessly told he was too busy for her stupid games. Of course, it could also be something more recent, but a good rule of thumb is that the deeper and stronger a particular reaction is felt, the earlier the memory that's associated with it. Regardless, one memory might come up, or several. Whatever emerges from your reflection will tell you, for better or worse, what your right brain is making of this present event.

PROCESSING THIS INFORMATION

I'll give you a step-by-step process for dealing with this information later in the book, but for now it's enough to ask yourself, "Do these specific memories really describe my present experience?" For instance, if Karen's right brain is taking her back to a time when she was bullied in grade school, she might ask if it's really fair to paint Julia with that same brush. If Julia has been mean or disrespectful in the past, it may very well be appropriate to lump her into the same category as the bullies in her past. But if not, it would be very unfair to assume that Julia is thinking about Karen the same way. Karen might not know what Julia is thinking, and Karen can now admit that. Rather than feel and act as if she is being aggressively shunned by Julia, she is free to look for another explanation that takes into account the way Julia has actually treated her in the past.

As I mentioned, we'll talk through what to do with all this information later on, but for now, it's important to become aware of these different layers of experience. The more anxious people are, the harder it is for them to get past even the first layer and hear their own self-talk, much less the memories that underlie their automatic interpretations. Those who experience serious anxiety tend to become so fixated on getting their external environment under control that they don't think to ask these questions. Because of this, much of their emotional experience remains unavailable, and they can't avoid the patterns that set them up for failure again and again.

Think about it. What would happen if Karen didn't ask herself these questions and eventually realize that it wasn't fair for her to automatically compare Julia to bullies in the past? Karen might avoid Julia in an attempt to protect herself from the imagined slight. Then Julia would probably be hurt because she wouldn't know why Karen didn't want to see her anymore, and she would stop trying to reach out. In fact, Julia might even complain to mutual friends about Karen's poor treatment of her, which could further jeopardize Karen's social position.

In response, Karen would experience all of this as proof that she truly is annoying and really does drive away everyone she cares about; and she would become even more anxious in future social situations. Imagine how crippling it would be if this same dynamic happened a thousand or even a hundred thousand times over the course of Karen's life. Our self-talk and memories have tremendous power to shape our experiences. It's important to become aware of these messages and memories — and exercise good stewardship over them — so that we can control them rather than allowing them to control us.

EXERCISE: Self-Talk Practice

To practice identifying the self-talk and memories that inform your unique experiences, take five minutes a day with your notebook to reflect on the following questions.

❏ What emotions am I feeling right now? Sad? Anxious? Happy? Hurt? Peaceful? Something else? Write down the feeling that best describes your experience.

❏ As you sit with that feeling, ask, "What thoughts are going through my mind as I feel these emotions?" Write down your answers.

❏ Finally, "As I sit with these feelings and thoughts, what memories come to the surface?" Write these down in your notebook.

Five minutes a day reflecting on your feelings — even if you're not feeling anything particularly earth-shattering (and it's better for this exercise if you aren't) — will train your mind to stop automatically attributing your feelings to what is happening to you, and help you begin to understand the many factors that influence your emotions. The point of this exercise is not to change anything, but to become aware of the information that will make change possible.

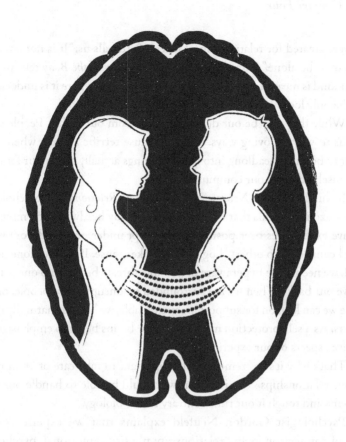

CHAPTER FOUR

You're Making Me Crazy — Relationships and Anxiety

We were created for relationships. Genesis 2:18 tells us, "It is not good for the man to be alone." Saint John Paul II's *Theology of the Body* tells us that humankind is meant to live in a "Civilization of Love," where it is understood that the only logical response to each person we meet is love.

While that may be our destiny, it is far from our reality. People often treat us in very unloving ways. This can cause terrific anxiety when what "ought to be" runs headlong into the way things actually are in our families, our households, and our communities.

In his book *The Neuroscience of Human Relationships*, psychologist Louis Cozolino reveals that our brains are actually hardwired to emphasize negative experiences over positive ones except under one condition: when we feel connected to others. Logically, it makes sense. If we are alone in the world, we need to be hyperaware of possible threats because no one is there to have our back. When we are surrounded by unsupportive people, or the people we can lean on for support are unavailable, we become naturally more anxious. As a self-protection mechanism, our brains begin to emphasize the negative aspects of our experience.

That's why it's so tremendously important to take care of and prioritize our relationships. The idea that we should be able to handle our own problems and tough it out runs contrary to our biology.

Psychologist Gordon Neufeld explains that we experience five types of connection in any relationship: physical, emotional, psychological, spiritual, and social. Of these, **physical connection** is the most intense form of connection, even though it has the shortest-lasting impact. Physical connection has to do with any kind of physical affection one person experiences with another. Physical connection has the strongest immediate impact on our ability to feel connected (and therefore less anxious), both because of the release of oxytocin, a powerful calm-down hormone associated with bonding, and because bodies in close proximity tend to sync up with each other. If an anxious person is lovingly held by someone who is calm and appropriately affectionate, the hug will stimulate the anxious person's parasympathetic (calm-down) nervous system. This enables them to re-regulate their body as the anxious person's heart rate, respiration, and other bodily systems synch up to that of the calmer person hugging them. Our bodies speak to each other in subtle but powerful ways.

Unfortunately, the effect of physical affection doesn't last long. As soon as the physical signs of affection are withdrawn, or the supportive people have to attend to their own affairs, the anxious person may have a harder time re-regulating themselves. As a result, the anxious person can become needy, jealous, or manipulative in an attempt to get their attachment figures to stay nearby and help them maintain their equilibrium. That's why it's so important to cultivate other, less intense but longer-acting, forms of connection.

For Reflection: *What is one simple and appropriate way you could strengthen the physical connection you have with a person who is important to you?*

Emotional Connection may not be felt as intensely as physical affection, but it tends to have a much longer shelf-life for helping to fight anxiety. Emotional connection refers to our ability to feel truly understood by the people around us. If a person who may not agree with us still takes the time to understand where we're coming from, express concern for our needs, and respect our feelings, we can say that we have a strong emotional attachment to that person. Emotional connection allows us to feel that people "get" us, like we belong to a group we can count on. That feeling of belonging produced by emotional connection persists even when the people aren't available to us. Knowing that there are people in the world who really understand us makes us feel more connected and, therefore, less anxious.

Cultivating emotional attachment involves learning how to both communicate your feelings and listen empathically. Empathic listening requires you to make conscious connections between the feelings another person is describing and the analogous feelings you have had in similar situations (while being careful not to make it all about you). When you do this, you are attempting to give yourself a glimpse of their inner world so that you can respond accordingly.

For example, if your friend says, "I was so excited when I got the promotion! I really wasn't expecting it."

You might empathically respond by first intentionally calling to mind a time you received unexpected recognition, remembering how you felt, and then saying, "Oh, my gosh! That's amazing, *you must have felt really proud of yourself, and grateful to be appreciated like that.*"

If you did a good job connecting your experience and feeling to theirs, your friend will probably respond with a slightly surprised look and say, "That's *exactly* how I felt! I'm really grateful to work at a place that recognizes how hard I worked on that account."

For Reflection: What is one simple thing you could do to strengthen your emotional connection with a person who is important to you?

Psychological connection is the connection we feel with others when we admire them for certain skills and traits and wish to imitate and be identified with them. Marriage researchers Drs. John and Julie Gottman refer to this as a "fondness and admiration system," and it is a fundamental building block in what they call a "sound relationship house."

Mutual fondness and admiration help affirm us in who we are today and challenge us to be even better people tomorrow. For instance, in the movie *As Good as It Gets*, Jack Nicolson plays an anxiety-ridden, obsessive-compulsive, verbally abusive misanthrope who tells Helen Hunt's character, "You make me want to be a better man." He is acknowledging the psychological attachment between them that makes him want to be more compliant with his psychiatric treatment, so that he could be worthy to be her friend. This drive to improve ourselves out of admiration for another and the desire to be associated with them sticks around even when that person can't be near us for a time.

Cultivating psychological attachment involves actively recognizing and verbally acknowledging each other's gifts and talents. It demonstrates an eagerness to learn from each other, a willingness to be influenced by each other, and a desire to grow and stretch (in healthy ways) for the sake of each other, even when you might prefer not to.

Think of someone you love. What do you admire about them? In what ways do you wish you were more like them? When you see something that interests or amuses you, do you ever think, "So-and-so would LOVE this!" Have you ever struggled with a problem and said to this person, "How would YOU handle thus and such?" These are all examples of the psychological attachment you have with that person.

For Reflection: What is one simple, concrete thing you could do today to strengthen your psychological connection with a person who is important to you?

Spiritual connection, in the broadest sense, means that you recognize that you and another person share a bigger purpose than just your relationship: a common vision for life, a common set of values, a common cause. Spiritual connection comes from the sense that you and another person (or group of people) were meant to be together, not because of any selfish reasons, but because you can see your relationship making a positive difference in the lives of the people around you and helping you experience more meaning in life. Examples of spiritual connection include the feelings you get when you see that you are raising great kids together, finding ways to share and promote your faith and values, or working together to effect positive changes in your community. Cultivating spiritual connection means looking for ways you and the people you are closest to can make some kind of difference in the world — together.

For Reflection: What is one, simple, concrete thing you could do today to increase your spiritual connection with a person who is important to you?

Finally, **social connection** has to do with the friends, activities, experiences, and groups you have in common. Research by Dr. Gary Lewandowski at Monmouth University suggests that social attachment lends a sense of relevance to a relationship. That is to say, it makes sense that you're together because you have so much in common. Social connection gives you a common experiential vocabulary that allows you to finish each other's sentences and get each other's inside jokes. When you're alone, social connection also makes you keep mental lists of things you can't wait to share with the other. Cultivating social connection involves being willing to leave behind your own comfort zone to cheerfully seek the truth, goodness, and beauty in the activities and relationships your friend finds true, good, and beautiful.

For Reflection: What is one simple thing you could do today to strengthen your social connection with a person who is important to you?

THE FIVE TYPES OF CONNECTION AND ANXIETY

Remember, our brains are hard-wired to be more anxious when we feel disconnected from others. By contrast, the stronger our link to someone across these five domains of physical, emotional, psychological, spiritual, and social connectedness, the more relaxed we will naturally feel. It can be extremely helpful for the person who struggles with anxiety to consider, in each of their relationships, what kinds of connection are strongest and what kinds need some work. Often, when I ask people — especially married people — to tell me about their relationships, they will say, "It's fine." When I press a little harder, they reveal that they mean that the relationship is the source of little conflict, but it is also often the source of very little intimacy or connection. Describing these types of connection allows people to say, "I have a strong social attachment with Bill, a pretty good physical connection with my wife, a solid psychological connection with my boss who is really more of a mentor to me, but I don't really have much of an emotional or spiritual connection with anyone."

If you struggle with anxiety, the more effort you can put into increasing all the different dimensions of connection you have — both *within* each relationship and *across* all your relationships — the more you will be able to enjoy the stress-busting power of your relationships.

ATTACHMENT STYLES

There is an even more fundamental way relationships affect the level of anxiety we feel. The phrase "attachment style" refers to our basic, gut-level assumptions, established within the first three to five years of life, about the way relationships work, how safe the world is, what we can rightly expect from others, and what others can rightly expect from us. There are three primary attachment styles: secure, anxious, and avoidant. A fourth, disorganized, is rarer, so we will not deal with it in this book.

To understand the relationship between the types of physical, emotional, psychological, spiritual, and social connection we just discussed and the three attachment styles we'll review below, it can be helpful to think of the five different types of connection (physical, emotional, psychological, spiritual, and social) as tubes that deliver different types of warm feelings back and forth between two people. Your attachment style represents the degree to which there may (or may not) be blockages in each of the five metaphorical "tubes" connecting your heart to another's, making it difficult for you to experience all the benefits that would otherwise naturally result from these connections.

Secure Attachment

People with a secure attachment style are able to enjoy the full benefits of all five types of attachment. These individuals were raised by affectionate, emotionally intelligent parents who responded to their needs promptly, generously, and consistently. As children, securely attached people were helped to discover appropriate ways to express their needs and emotions and taught to give to others as generously as they received. People with a secure attachment style are comfortable both being independent and leaning on others. They are also comfortable having other people appropriately depend upon them. They have a generally positive view of the world and the sense that they are able to count on the support of others to set and achieve healthy life goals. People with a secure attachment style are prone to stress and anxiety when going through particularly difficult times but, in general, they are less prone to day-to-day anxiety and bounce back more quickly from stressful experiences. That's because a parent's prompt, generous, and consistent attention to a child's needs stimulates the child's calm-down nervous system, teaching the child to self-regulate in the presence of stressful events.

Incidentally, this prompt, generous, and consistent attention does not mean that the parent hovered or constantly did things for the child. Rather, it means that the parents were responsive to the child and taught the child healthy ways to meet his or her needs in collaboration with others. When the child was a baby, that meant responding quickly to cries and meeting the child's needs. But as the child got older, that same parent was good at helping the child identify and meet his or her own needs in a healthy and appropriate way. Through this process of secure attachment, the child learns that the world is a safe place filled with helpful people (if you know where to look), and that the child is competent to meet his or her own needs efficiently in most situations. The securely attached child grows up to be a calm, capable, and predominantly peaceful adult.

Anxious Attachment

People with an anxious attachment style are able to experience all five types of connection with others, but the "tubes" that convey this connection are partially blocked, leading the person to feel that even though they get enough emotional "oxygen" to survive, they are often gasping for air. People with anxious attachment usually felt they had to work a little harder to get their parents to respond to their emotional and affection needs. Perhaps the parents were anxious themselves, or they were afraid of "spoiling" the child with "too much" affection, so they intentionally withheld approval and affirmation from their children. Perhaps the parents were going through serious problems of their own that depleted their emotional resources and didn't leave them much energy to be nurturing toward their child. Regardless, children raised in such homes tend to grow up thinking that it is their job to make other people love them. It is simply too terrible for a child to believe that the people who are supposed to meet their emotional needs can't or won't. So, they focus their energy on pushing behavioral and emotional buttons in an attempt to get their parent to give them the love and affirmation they crave.

This dynamic leads people with an anxious attachment style to enter adulthood relationships assuming that it is their job to fix other people's unhappiness — even when they can't do anything about it. When they are unable to do so, they often feel terribly guilty, even if they know, intellectually, they have no reason to. They also tend to think that if a relationship isn't working — especially a romantic relationship — it must be their fault (especially when it is not). People with an anxious attachment style tend to fill their lives with people who can't love them properly and then blame themselves for simply not being worthy of the support they see other people getting. All of this causes them to be much more prone to experiencing a generalized sense of anxiety. That is, they feel anxious all the time, even when things seem to be going okay for them. Even though these folks are often highly competent and capable (they have to be so that they can handle all the responsibility of trying to make everyone around them happy all the time), they simply become worn out from always being on high alert. They live in constant fear that they might disappoint someone or let somebody down in some way — *and that would be terrible!*

Avoidant Attachment

Avoidantly attached people grew up in households where their physical needs were met, but very few of their emotional needs were attended to. They were taught from an early age that — emotionally speaking, at least — they were on their own. As such, most of the connection tubes are almost totally blocked for these individuals. Some avoidantly attached people grew up in households where they only received praise when they performed perfectly. These people grow up to be adults who get little pleasure from relationships (even when they have them) but can outperform anyone else in the workplace. They often hold positions of power and prominence but feel emotionally empty. Other avoidantly attached people discovered that even good performance went unrewarded. These folks grow up to focus simply on doing what must be done to get through the day. Avoidantly attached people feel burdened by relationships. They hate to depend on others and hate for others to depend on them. For them, a good relationship is one where people leave each other alone.

Avoidantly attached people are often unaware of their feelings in general. Anxiety tends to come out of nowhere and be all-consuming when it happens. Or, they tend to suffer from stress-related illnesses like irritable bowel syndrome and fibromyalgia — real, physical disorders often caused by the stress that results from poor parental and social attachment. People with avoidant attachment styles tend to have impaired awareness of how their emotional, relational, and spiritual lives are contributing to their anxiety. As such, they tend to rely too heavily on seeking both physical causes and cures for their anxiety. Because they have few psychological or relational resources to deal with these intense, intrusive emotions, they often turn to drink, drugs, or obsessive behaviors (like extreme exercise, extreme nutritional regimens/diets, scrupulosity, workaholism, gambling, compulsive pornography use, etc.) in an attempt to anesthetize themselves from emotional pain. This behavior allows them to function in the short-term, but long-term, makes the experience of anxiety worse as their personal and relational disasters pile up.

The good news is that if you are anxiously or avoidantly attached, you can learn to be more securely attached by developing healthy relationships with securely attached people. Although healthy relationships can make anxiously attached people suspicious ("Why are you so nice to me? What do you want from me?") and avoidantly attached people feel irritated ("Ugh. Stop wanting 'so much' from me!"), these relationships can teach you that you don't have to work so hard to get others to stick around, or to remember that it really is important to need others and be needed by them. It is hard work, and it doesn't come naturally, which is why therapy is often a necessary part of healing attachment wounds. Often, it is a crisis that makes the anxiously or avoidantly attached person see that something needs to change. But with proper attention, the crushing and constant sense of anxiety that accompanies these individuals' gut-level struggles to form healthy connections with others can be healed.

EXERCISE: Connection, Attachment, and Anxiety

As with other exercises in this book, it is incredibly important and helpful to take even five minutes each day to reflect on the degree of connection and strength of attachment you feel in your relationships. Sit in a quiet space, just for a few moments, and write down your answers to the following questions.

1. How close do you feel to the people in your life?
2. What is the strength of the physical, emotional, psychological, spiritual, or social connection you have with the most important people around you?
3. What is one small, even tiny, thing you can do — in the next few hours and whether or not you feel like it — to strengthen one dimension of

connectedness (i.e., physical, emotional, psychological, spiritual, or so-cial) with another person who shares your life?

This exercise will make you more aware of the impact of relationships in your overall sense of peace and anxiety and give you at least a thumbnail sketch of what you can begin to do about it. Remember, connection grows peace. Disconnection accelerates anxiety. Make a point to take even tiny, consistent, daily steps to cultivate rich, rewarding connections with the people around you. Challenge yourself to have meaningful conversations about your hopes and dreams, feelings, and needs. Stretch yourself to become a more affectionate, affirming person who is comfortable giving (and receiving) compliments. In other words, make creating real depth and intimacy a daily goal in your relationships. The more you do this, the more successful you will be at sending messages to your anxious brain that *it is not alone* — so you can be at peace.

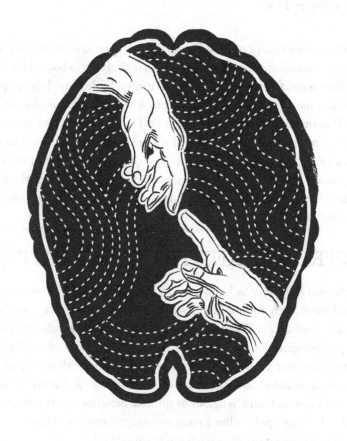

CHAPTER FIVE

My Anxious Spirit — Spirituality and Anxiety

In almost every study on the subject, faith has been shown to be a positive factor in decreasing anxiety, increasing a person's ability to bounce back from stressful events, facilitating physical and mental health, and helping people cultivate a more peaceful life. (The books *Religion and Coping* by Dr. Kenneth Pargament and *Faith and Health* by Dr. Thomas Plante present the most comprehensive examinations of the research on this subject to date.) Even so, faith can sometimes be toxic, and when it is, it often causes anxiety. The research shows that there are two primary conditions in which faith can be toxic to peace: when people's faith is extrinsic, and when they have insecure God-attachment.

EXTRINSIC AND INTRINSIC FAITH

People who have what is known as *extrinsic faith* tend to be more anxious — and more likely to find faith itself stress-inducing — than people who have an *intrinsic faith*. These two faith-styles were first identified by personality psychologist Gordon Allport.[1] Extrinsic faith is defined as religious or spiritual behavior primarily oriented to achieving non-religious goals such as parental or social acceptance, approval, or success and social status. By contrast, intrinsic faith is religious or spiritual behavior that is primarily oriented to helping a person live a more meaningful, integrated life.

The following are all examples of extrinsic faith:

+ A child who goes to church to please his or her parents.
+ A person who attends religious services because it is just something people of his or her ethnic/cultural background do.
+ A woman who goes to a particular place of worship because all of her friends in her mother's group attend that church.
+ A realtor who goes to church because it is a good way to get clients.

---

1   It is important to note that "faith" as it is used here refers to the individual's experience of faith. It is not the same as the theological virtue of faith, which is a supernatural gift that we cannot achieve through our own efforts. The theological virtue of faith can never be defective in itself, but our apprehension and appropriation of the gift of faith can be limited or impaired. This discussion of extrinsic and intrinsic faith, therefore, refers to ways that individuals experience faith, or religiosity.

In each of these examples, people engage in various religious practices, not because they find these practices personally meaningful or even because they agree with the beliefs and teachings represented by those practices, but because they hope to gain some non-religious, social, cultural, or economic benefit by their participation.

Extrinsic faith is not always stressful, but it often is, because the person with extrinsic faith sees spiritual practices as a means to an end. Most of their spiritual efforts are geared either toward using religious practices to gain approval/acceptance or achieve some other personal benefit. For those who are reluctant to give approval in general, or whose practical goals and wishes are frustrated, extrinsic faith will tend to be either scrupulous (in an attempt to manipulate the spiritual system that's allied against them) or frustrated and angry (because God isn't playing by their rules). If they can't resolve this emotional tension, they may eventually come to dismiss faith as just one more obstacle in the way of meeting their real (unconscious and unstated) primary goals of approval, affirmation, social acceptance, or professional success

Rebecca was a new mom who began attending a mother's support group. Though she'd never considered herself a particularly religious person, she liked the other women in the group and felt that much of the advice they shared was helpful. Unfortunately, many of the women tended to be somewhat dogmatic in their approach to parenting. They often stated that to be a "good Christian mother" one needed to engage in specific parenting practices. Mothers who struggled to live up to the group's standards did not receive support or understanding in their struggles, but rather were labeled as "lazy" or "worldly." Rebecca felt trapped. She really liked these women and they formed the basis of her entire social network. She didn't want to leave, but the more she associated with the group, the more she felt that she was failing her family, her friends, her church, and ultimately God when she could not follow the group's particular parenting standards to the letter. Rebecca found herself constantly second-guessing her choices, feeling judged even when no one else was around, and lying awake nights wondering what was wrong with her.

As you can see, extrinsic faith can be sincere in its way, but it is often a poor source of comfort because, unlike intrinsic faith, it is not intended to help you make more sense out of your life. Rather, it is intended to get another person to give you something you do not feel you can claim for yourself (self-esteem, social/cultural identity, professional success). If Rebecca's faith had been more intrinsic than extrinsic, things might have played out differently. For instance:

Rebecca was a new mom who began attending a mother's support group. She'd never considered herself a particularly religious person, she liked the other women in the group and felt that much of the advice they shared was helpful. In the course of attending the group, sometimes she found the other women to be a bit militant in their opinions. Instead of relying on the other women to tell her what her church taught, she took it upon herself to learn more about her faith. When what she learned — either on her own or from the other women in her group — didn't mesh with her experience, she didn't reject it, but she didn't beat herself up about it either. She trusted that if it was true, she would grow into it in time. Instead, she focused on doing her best to take what she could from the group and, using that support as a springboard, to become more involved with her faith and the church in which she found comfort. She tried to be a positive influence in her group and the church, to pray more on her own and learn more about her faith, and to let God lead her step-by-step down the path that made the most sense for her and her family. It wasn't always easy, and some of the more petty women in the group did make life difficult for her from time to time, but her own relationship with God helped her keep her bearings — and her faith — in these situations.

In the beginning, everyone's faith is extrinsic. As children and/or newcomers to the faith, we learn religious beliefs and practices from others. However, at some point (for most people, in adolescence), we each have to decide whether our faith is a series of hoops we will jump through to gain the approval of others — parents, our culture, or our social group — or a source of meaning, integration, transformation, and transcendence in our lives.

No one can give us intrinsic faith. As my wife and I point out in our book *Discovering God Together: The Catholic Guide to Raising Faithful Kids*, parents (and other significant figures in our lives) can invite children to own their faith by presenting it as the legitimate source of the warmth in the relationship. But until it is owned as a personal source of meaning, integration, transformation, and transcendence, faith will remain extrinsic. While it is beyond my scope here to show you in detail how to move from a more extrinsic to a more intrinsic experience of faith, I can tell you that the process begins by asking God to show himself to you in a real and personal way. If you would like to experience your faith as a source of greater peace and wholeness in your life, I would invite you to pray something like the following prayer. Feel free to use your own words but bring your whole heart to the experience.

> Lord, the way I have been living — and, in particular, living my faith — isn't working for me anymore. I come before you now, and I ask you to help me love you with my whole heart, mind, soul, and strength. Let your Holy Spirit come alive in me. Let me meet you in the sacraments, listen to you in your word, and know you in my heart. Take everything I have and everything I am: my talents, my gifts, my life, my work, and my concerns. I ask only that you love me and teach me to love you in return. Through Jesus Christ our Lord. Amen.

Of course, this is just the beginning. You will need to approach your faith differently from now on. When you are at Mass, don't just go through the motions. Ask God to help you find him in the Eucharist. When you hear or read Scripture, prayerfully ask God what he is saying to you through the words. When you pray, don't just say words at God. Bring your whole self to it, rededicate your life and your relationships to him, and ask for the grace to be his disciple in all you do. And, of course, take a little time each day to learn more about what it means to love and be loved by him. Books like *Rediscover Jesus* and *Rediscover Catholicism* by Matthew Kelly and *Fruitful Discipleship* by Sherry Weddell are terrific resources that can help you on the road to experiencing the peace that this world cannot give — the peace that only comes from a sincere, personal relationship with Christ. The more your faith becomes intrinsic, the more you will be able to put aside your anxiety, sit at the feet of the Lord, and let your heart be still, knowing that he is God.

INSECURE GOD-ATTACHMENT

Even for people who do experience a more personal, intrinsic faith, there is another factor that can sometimes prevent a person from experiencing the full benefits of life in Christ: insecure attachment to God.

In the last chapter, I described the different attachment styles (secure, anxious, and avoidant) that comprise a person's gut-level, unconscious assumptions about how relationships work, how safe it is to trust others, how much it is appropriate to depend on others and have them depend on you, and how much enjoyment and support one can feel from being in the company of others. Recall that secure attachment allows the full emotional benefits of connection to flow freely between any two people. By contrast, insecure attachment represents kinks or blockages in the metaphorical tubes that allow people to fully experience the physical, emotional, psychological, spiritual, and social connectedness relationship provides (and the peace that attends such a multidimensional connection).

These attachment styles influence all of our relationships, both with other human beings and with God. Our attachment style determines how close we can feel to God and how much strength and peace we will experience in our relationship with God.

People with secure God-attachment experience God as a loving, forgiving, supportive presence in their lives. For the most part, they are comfortable being completely honest in their prayer lives, willing to admit their faults, and open about the times that they feel angry, sad, frustrated, doubtful, or disappointed with God. They are confident that God will deal with them in loving, merciful ways, and that he is intent upon working for their good and leading them into deeper communion with him, even when life is hard or confusing.

ANXIOUS GOD-ATTACHMENT

People with anxious God-attachment, even when they have an intrinsic faith, tend to worry about disappointing God or not being worthy of his love. Of course, strictly speaking, none of us deserves God's love, but despite this he has promised that he loves us unfailingly. The securely God-attached person can be at peace with the fact that God loves them despite their imperfections and can seek God's forgiveness, confident in his willingness to forgive them and welcome them back. But the anxiously God-attached person is never completely sure — on a personal level — that God really meant what he said when he promised never to leave us or forsake us (cf. Heb 13:5). Wrestling with doubt is a normal part of faith. But the anxiously God-attached person can't help but harbor persistent, anxiety-producing doubts about the limits of God's patience and faithfulness, not because of any flaw on God's part, but because they are so painfully aware of their own flaws. The anxiously God-attached person may tend toward scrupulosity and self-recrimination, worrying that their sins and failings are a constant source of disappointment for a God who is more of an angry judge than a Divine Physician and Good Shepherd. Even when a person has an intrinsic faith, if they are anxiously God-attached, they may find it difficult to be honest in prayer, only focusing on properly thanking and honoring God, while failing to ask him for help with the messier parts of their life. If they do ask for God's assistance, it tends to be in the spirit of a child who expects to be smacked by his parent for asking too much or wearing out his patience. While every person might deal with some of these fears from time to time, this insecurity is the heart of the anxiously God-attached person's relationship with God.

Because of this, even drawing close to God can be a source of anxiety. As good as closeness with God feels, there is the sense that it is only a matter of time before God gives up on them and withdraws. This can lead the anxiously attached person to focus more on their own imperfect efforts than on God's love and mercy. They can become stuck in their spiritual walk, for fear of disappointing God, because of their reluctance to honestly confront doubts and questions about their faith.

Just as anxious attachment in human relationships can be healed with counseling and the experience of healthy, stable, loving relationships, anxious God-attachment can be similarly healed with spiritual direction or pastoral counseling and faithful adherence to religious practice, combined with active reflection on God's love and providence. Keeping a gratitude journal can be a particularly useful exercise for the anxiously God-attached person. Take a few minutes each day to write down the little blessings of that day — especially the good things that happened that you didn't initially think to attribute to God. The fact is, God is the source of all good things. If you experienced a blessing today, it came from him. Write it down. As you write, take a moment to thank God for that blessing. Know that his generosity is not due to your perfection or your worthiness, but to his mercy, which is as constant as it is undeserved. Praise him for it! Let every blessing you experienced be a sign to you of the free, total, faithful, and fruitful love God has for you. With each blessing, say a little prayer like, "Thank you, Lord, for your abundant love. Jesus, I trust in you." Then, go back over the blessing you wrote down for the last few weeks and praise God for each one in a similar way.

Devotion to Saint Faustina Kowalska and the Divine Mercy can be a very healing spiritual practice for the anxiously God-attached person. Saint Faustina's writings are a reminder that despite our weaknesses, God is ever faithful, ever loving, ever patient, and ever merciful. "Let no one doubt concerning the goodness of God; even if a person's sins were as dark as night, God's mercy is stronger than our misery. One thing alone is necessary; that the sinner set ajar the door of his heart, be it ever so little, to let in a ray of God's merciful grace, and then God will do the rest."

For additional ideas for healing attachment wounds that affect the peace you can encounter in your relationship with God, see *God Attachment* by Dr. Tim Clinton.

AVOIDANT GOD-ATTACHMENT

Where the person with avoidant attachment tends to view relationships as an inconvenience if not an outright stumbling-block to happiness, the avoidantly God-attached person is likely to see God as optional. If the avoidantly attached person develops an intrinsic faith (which is difficult but not impossible), it will probably be more dutiful and contractual in nature. That is, the avoidantly God-attached person tends to see his relationship to God as a tit-for-tat exchange: they agree to say certain prayers, participate in certain rituals, and live a certain way, with the understanding that God will do certain things for them in return. For the avoidantly God-attached person, faith is more of an arrangement than a real relationship.

Serious spiritual and psychological angst can result if God fails to hold up his end of the "bargain." Such "behavior" on God's part (experienced as loss or frustrations in the person's life) often triggers much deeper wounds in the person, reminding them of all the ways their early caregivers were not there for them and making them feel foolish for trusting that anyone — especially God — would truly come through. This can be a source of tremendous anxiety, as it makes the avoidantly attached person feel utterly and entirely alone and inclined toward addictive and compulsive behaviors in an attempt to cope with that loneliness.

The problem with this perception of God, of course, is that God is not a vending machine. We do not pay him with prayers and religious practices to get goodies in return. We have a relationship with him because we know his love for us and therefore we love him back. The avoidantly God-attached person struggles with this concept, just as they struggle with the idea of being vulnerable to or intimate with anyone.

Of course, avoidant God-attachment can be healed through pastoral counseling, and a willingness to remain faithful in one's religious practices without expecting to get "paid back" combined with a willingness to do what is necessary to become more spiritually, emotionally, and psychologically connected to all the people in his or her life. Avoidantly attached people have a hard enough time relating in an intimate, authentic way to people they can see, much less a God they can't. But the more they cultivate their capacity for intimacy on a human level while maintaining their religious practices, the more the intimacy they create with others will spill over into their relationship with God as well (and vice-versa). Again, the book *God Attachment* by Tim Clinton and pastoral counseling through organizations like the Pastoral Solutions Institute can be tremendously helpful for allowing the avoidantly God-attached person to open their heart to the peace and grace one can only experience in an intimate, personal relationship with God.

If you are wondering how your God attachment style might be affecting your ability to enjoy the anxiety-proofing benefits of faith, take the following quiz developed by Dr. R. Beck and Dr. A. MacDonald and published in the *Journal of Psychology and Theology* (2004). It is not a diagnostic tool, but an instrument to evaluate your capacity to enjoy a healthy, stable, and healing relationship with God.

EXERCISE: Attachment to God Inventory

Directions: Circle the number that indicates your level of agreement from Disagree Strongly (DS) to Neutral (N) to Agree Strongly (AS). The points assigned will vary from question to question. Don't worry about the numbers for now, just view them as place-holders that indicate your level of agreement/disagreement with each question.

1. My experiences with God are very intimate and emotional.

```
        DS ————— N ————— AS
         7    6    5    4    3    2    1
```

2. I prefer not to depend too much on God.

```
        DS ————— N ————— AS
         1    2    3    4    5    6    7
```

3. My prayers to God are very emotional.

```
        DS ————— N ————— AS
         7    6    5    4    3    2    1
```

4. I am totally dependent upon God for everything in my life.

```
        DS ————— N ————— AS
         7    6    5    4    3    2    1
```

5. Without God I couldn't function at all.

```
        DS ————— N ————— AS
         7    6    5    4    3    2    1
```

6. I just don't feel a deep need to be close to God.

                DS ————— N ————— AS

                   1   2   3   4   5   6   7

7. Daily I discuss all of my problems and concerns with God.

                DS ————— N ————— AS

                   7   6   5   4   3   2   1

8. I am uncomfortable allowing God to control every aspect of my life.

                DS ————— N ————— AS

                   1   2   3   4   5   6   7

9. I let God make most of the decisions in my life.

                DS ————— N ————— AS

                   7   6   5   4   3   2   1

10. I am uncomfortable with emotional displays of affection to God.

                DS ————— N ————— AS

                   1   2   3   4   5   6   7

11. It is uncommon for me to cry when sharing with God.

                DS ————— N ————— AS

                   1   2   3   4   5   6   7

12. I am uncomfortable being emotional in my communication with God.

                DS ————— N ————— AS

                   1   2   3   4   5   6   7

13. I believe people should not depend on God for things they should do for themselves.

                DS ————— N ————— AS

                   1   2   3   4   5   6   7

14. My prayers to God are often matter-of-fact and not very personal.

DS ————— N ————— AS

1   2   3   4   5   6   7

Subtotal Scale 1 (Questions 1–14) _____

15. I worry a lot about my relationship with God.

DS ————— N ————— AS

1   2   3   4   5   6   7

16. I often worry about whether God is pleased with me.

DS ————— N ————— AS

1   2   3   4   5   6   7

17. I get upset when I feel God helps others but forgets about me.

DS ————— N ————— AS

1   2   3   4   5   6   7

18. I fear God does not accept me when I do wrong.

DS ————— N ————— AS

1   2   3   4   5   6   7

19. I often feel angry with God for not responding to me.

DS ————— N ————— AS

1   2   3   4   5   6   7

20. I worry a lot about damaging my relationship with God.

DS ————— N ————— AS

1   2   3   4   5   6   7

21. I am jealous at how God seems to care more for others than for me.

DS ————— N ————— AS

1   2   3   4   5   6   7

22. I am jealous when others feel God's presence when I cannot.

DS ————— N ————— AS

1   2   3   4   5   6   7

23. I am jealous at how close some people are to God.

DS ————— N ————— AS

1   2   3   4   5   6   7

24. If I can't see God working in my life, I get upset or angry.

DS ————— N ————— AS

1   2   3   4   5   6   7

25. Sometimes I feel that God loves others more than me.

DS ————— N ————— AS

1   2   3   4   5   6   7

26. Almost daily I feel that my relationship with God goes back and forth from "hot" to "cold."

DS ————— N ————— AS

1   2   3   4   5   6   7

27. I crave reassurance from God that God loves me.

DS ————— N ————— AS

1   2   3   4   5   6   7

28. Even if I fail, I never question that God is pleased with me.

DS ————— N ————— AS

7   6   5   4   3   2   1

Subtotal Scale 2 (Questions 15–28) _____

Grand Total of Scales 1 & 2 (All Questions) _____

Scoring

Step 1: Add up the points for all the questions (Note: Some scoring is reversed). This is your **Overall Attachment to God Score.** This score sug-gests how secure your relationship with God is overall. The lower the score the better. The lowest possible score is a 28 (1 point per question), which would indicate an "Absolutely Secure" relationship with God. A score of 56 or less still indicates a "Very Secure" relationship with God. Scores higher than 57 (up to a maximum of 196) indicate varying degrees of insecurity in your relationship with God. That insecurity could cause you to be more anxious about your relationship with God than you ought to be or more avoidant in your relationship with God than you ought to be. Steps 2 and 3 will help you determine whether avoidance or anxiety is more responsible for the degree of insecurity you display.

Step 2: Add questions 1–14. Write the total on "Subtotal Scale 1." This is your score for the **Avoidant Scale.**

The lower the score the better. The lowest possible score is 14 which would indicate that you are not at all avoidant in your relationship with God. In other words, you feel absolutely eager to share your thoughts, feel-ings, hopes, and dreams with God and rely on him in every aspect of your life.

A score of 28 or less suggests that you are generally very comfortable sharing your thoughts, feelings, hopes, and dreams with God and relying on him in every aspect of your life.

A score of 29 or higher means that there may be several ways you tend to resist sharing your heart with God or relying on him in parts of your life.

The higher your Avoidant Scale score, the more obstacles you tend to put up between yourself and God and the harder it is for you to let him influence your life and relationships. The maximum possible score on the Avoidant Scale is 98.

Step 3: Add questions 15–28. Write the total on "Subtotal Scale 2." This is your score for the **Anxious Scale.**

The lower the score the better. The lowest possible score is 14, which would indicate that you are absolutely confident and trusting in your re-lationship with God. In other words, you never doubt or question God's mercy, providence, or caring/nurturing presence in your life.

A score of 28 or less suggests that you rarely doubt or question God's mercy, providence, or caring/nurturing presence in your life.

A score of 29 or higher means that you tend to worry that God may not always be there for you, that you might behave in ways that could cause him to abandon you, or that somehow he might forget about you and your needs.

The higher your Anxious Scale score, the stronger your anxiety is about God either forgetting/abandoning you or alienating him with even simple mistakes/errors in judgment (i.e., scrupulosity). The maximum possible score on the Anxious Scale is 98.

Remember, your score on this instrument is not intended to be diagnostic of any mental health problem, neither is it intended to be an indictment of your relationship with God. Rather, it merely indicates challenges you may experience in your relationship with God. The higher your scores on the anxious and avoidant God-attachment scales, the more difficult it may be for you to experience your faith as a source of peace, security, and comfort no matter how sincere and deeply held it may be.

If you are unhappy with the results of this inventory, don't despair. Later in this book, we'll explore additional spiritual resources that can help you fight anxiety by maintaining a closer connection with God. In the meantime, keep up whatever religious and spiritual practices are meaningful for you, but seek out resources that can help you in healing your attachment wound. Learn to let faith be the source of the warmth in your heart, allowing you to experience the peace of God that is beyond all understanding and the source of incredible strength amid the storms of life.

CHAPTER SIX

Body Language

In the first chapters of this book, you discovered that anxiety begins as a physical experience. The anxious person tends to externalize their response to anxiety. That is, they tend to look for external things they can control in an attempt to increase their internal peace. This results in a game I like to call the "If I can justs."

> "If I can just finish this project, I'll be fine."
> "If I can just get my marriage back on track, I won't be so nervous anymore."
> "If I can just help my kids handle X crisis better, I'll feel better."
> "If I can just bring in a little more money, I wouldn't have to worry all the time."
> "If I can just … (fill in your own blank)."

It's not that any of these goals are bad. In fact, finishing your projects, getting your marriage in order, helping your kids succeed, and/or being able to meet your financial obligations are all tremendously important parts of combatting anxiety, just as having a pile of uncompleted projects, suffering from a breakup, watching your kids struggle, and dealing with money problems can add to your stress. But as you have already discovered, anxiety actually inhibits your brain's ability to respond effectively to life's problems. Instead, you simply react, which makes you feel powerless and usually makes the problems bigger in the long run, which increases your experience of anxiety.

The first step in controlling anxiety is not solving the problems outside of you; it is learning to regulate your physical reaction to anxiety. This approach is counterintuitive, but treating this as your first step will enable you to stop living in reaction. Adopting this approach will allow your thinking brain (your cortex) to come back online so that you can respond, rather than react, to the stressors in your life.

In his *Theology of the Body*, Saint John Paul II reminds us that we can discern a great deal about God's intentions for the way we live and relate to others by reflecting upon the way he designed our bodies. Reflecting on the stress-management mechanisms God built into your body can teach you to cooperate with his grace and experience greater peace in your life. In this chapter, we will focus on simple, powerful strategies that can help you stop being a victim of your body's reaction to stress. I will show you how you can start to take control of your body's stress response so that, regardless of what life throws at you, you will be able to process it efficiently and effectively.

YOUR SURGE-PROTECTION NETWORK

Despite how we feel when we fall prey to anxiety, God designed us to be incredibly anxiety-resistant. By understanding how our bodies work, we can more effectively cooperate with our God-given natural resources so we can respond to his grace and be freed from the tyranny of stress. To understand why learning to get control of your bodily reactions to stress is so important to overcoming anxiety, it can be helpful to think of your body as a surge protector.

A surge protector allows you to plug several appliances or components of a computer or entertainment system into one outlet. But it has a second, even more important function. It prevents electrical spikes in the power lines — caused by lightning, power outages, or other factors — from burning out your equipment. If the power to your house spikes either because of some natural event or something like the restoration of power after an outage, the surge protector will detect the increased voltage coming into your equipment and redirect it to a grounding wire, preventing damage to the expensive equipment you have plugged into it. A good-quality surge protector can redirect a surprising amount of power and save thousands of dollars of complicated, sensitive equipment.

Your body is like a giant surge protector, intended to protect your cortex (your thinking brain, arguably the most "expensive" piece of equipment in your body) from being overloaded by the spikes in stress you may encounter throughout life. When our bodies are working at their peak capacity, we can go through a host of very stressful, even traumatic events, and still be able to process and respond to that stress. In fact, because life is complex, and because stressors come at us from many different directions at one time, each of us has several built-in surge protectors designed to ground us in times of stress. For the most part, the body is the first line of defense, but if its surge protectors get overloaded, then a secondary set of surge protectors, made up of mental, relational, and spiritual resources, kick in to further diffuse the stress and decrease the voltage of the emotional shock to your system. This allows you to absorb the stress rather than be overrun by it and permits your cortex to respond to the stressor in an appropriate, proportionate, and productive manner. Ultimately, this process enables you to take small, effective steps to overcome your external stressors, such as job stress, financial pressures, life circumstances, and all the rest.

The more surges these protectors take, the more you feel threatened — even in the absence of an actual, imminent threat — and the more your fear-activation system kicks in. As we discussed at the beginning of the book, this system is housed in your limbic system. It engages when your bodily, psychological, relational, and spiritual surge protectors are overwhelmed and the high voltage stress-spike comes at your cortex (your thinking-brain) like a lightning bolt. To protect itself, your brain powers down the cortex and all your precious problem-solving and thinking resources and redirects the energy to your limbic system, which engages your fight, flight, or freeze response. This cortical shut-down, combined with the activation of your fight/flight/freeze response, prevents you from overthinking the perceived imminent threat and sends a powerful jolt of energy through your body motivating you to do one of three things:

1. Attack the thing you think is attacking you.
2. Run away.
3. Become effectively paralyzed, focusing your energy on avoiding the problem, or, under extreme circumstances, shutting down entirely ("going blank"), in the hopes that the threat will go away if you just keep your head down.

This fear-threat response system is tremendously helpful for enabling you to escape immediate dangers to your safety or wellbeing, but it is not designed to help you solve problems. Anxiety is the result of this fear-threat system becoming too easily activated, either because the physical, psychological, relational, and spiritual "surge protectors" were not installed properly in the first place (usually because you grew up in an inadequately affectionate/affirming family of origin), or because unusually traumatic life-events have fried the various surge protectors, and your body directs all stress immediately to the cortical shut-down system, or some combination of the two. In either case, anxiety results.

The next several chapters will examine ways you can rebuild and reinstall a more sophisticated surge-protection network. You'll be able to diffuse and absorb even the highest voltage stress spikes in your life and maintain your sense of peace and control.

YOUR BODY: THE FIRST SURGE-PROTECTOR

There are many ways you can consciously strengthen your body's surge protecting power. In fact, for the Christian, it can be helpful to realize that God speaks to us in many different ways. One of those ways is through the language of the body. By learning to listen to our bodies, we can hear God saying things like, "I need you to pace yourself," or, "How about a nap?" Or even, "I would like you to eat healthier and exercise a bit more." God tells us these things through our bodies so that we can be strong, healthy people capable of serving him and each other with all our heart, mind, and strength.

We reviewed some simple but powerful strategies for boosting your body's stress-fighting capacity in an earlier chapter, like consciously slowing down your rate of speech and actions, and thoughtful breathing. In addition to this, several other good habits can help you upgrade your body's stress-diffusing ability. These include important but often overlooked things like regular sleep, exercise, nutrition and supplements, and, in some cases, medication.

SLEEP

Inadequate sleep can seriously impact the body's ability to serve as an effective stress surge protector. According to the National Sleep Foundation, people need between seven and nine hours of sleep per night for the body to fully heal, recharge, and restore its natural stress-fighting abilities. A person who is not especially stressed may function passably with less sleep, but the person who is going through a particularly anxious time, or who is naturally more anxious, is going to need more sleep to function just as well.

Among many other benefits, in the deepest stages of sleep (N3 and REM), hormones are secreted that heal tissue damage and reduce cortisol levels caused by stress. Decreasing cortisol helps to reset the body's baseline stress level, making it more difficult for life events to trigger the body's fear-threat response. An article in the journal *Neural Plasticity* reported that during sleep the brain integrates learning and memory more effectively, which enables people to adapt to stress more effectively. The same article reported that sleep facilitates the formation of new neural connections in the brain that help diffuse the additional "load" placed on the nervous system by stressful events. As a rule, the more stressful we feel our lives are, the more sleep we need, and the more our bodies tell us to prioritize the habits that produce good quality sleep.

According to the Anxiety and Depression Association of America, some habits that promote healthy sleep include:

+ Establish a regular bedtime routine. About an hour before bed, turn off all electronics.
+ Take some time reflect and journal about the events of the day or read quietly, listen to soft music, and take your time getting ready for bed.
+ Avoid caffeine several hours before bed.
+ Stop work at least an hour before bed. This includes housework and bill paying.
+ Engage in regular, light exercise. However, do not exercise too close to attempting sleep. Leave at least an hour between completing exercise and going to bed.
+ Do not work in your bedroom. Make your bedroom a safe space. Save it for sleeping and relaxing only.
+ A cool, dark room is better than a warm room for quality sleep. Be careful to eliminate as much light as possible. Cover various LED's

with black electrical tape.

+ Avoid looking at the clock. Once you're in bed, don't worry about how long it might be taking to fall asleep. Resting of any kind is good. Make yourself comfortable. Keep your eyes closed. Focus on your breathing and relaxing your body. Don't force sleep. Let it come.

In addition, a study by Baylor University found that writing out a list of things to be done the next day and developing even a simple plan for getting them done (even if that plan subsequently changed) allowed people to fall asleep significantly faster than simply journaling about the day's events or not writing at all. One of the main reasons anxious people report sleep problems is that ruminating about responsibilities often keeps them awake. Writing out a simple plan of attack can convince the brain that you're on top of things enough to let you get the rest you need to handle the next day.

Finally, prayer can be a wonderful way to prepare for restful sleep. Don't feel guilty about falling asleep while praying. Remember, Saint Thérèse of Lisieux once said that just as a surgeon puts his patients to sleep before operating, the Divine Physician often puts his patients to sleep when he intends to work the deepest change. Instead of fighting your drowsiness during nighttime prayer, remember when you used to fall asleep in your mother's arms. Rest in God. Bring him your concerns. Ask God to hold you close to his heart. Focus on your breathing. Thank God for caring for you and providing each breath you take. Every time you exhale, say (in your head) "Jesus, I trust in you." Fall asleep in the arms of the God who loves you and provides for all of your needs.

EXERCISE

We love to hate it, but it would be a mistake to underestimate the role that exercise plays in helping to upgrade the body's ability to be an effective anti-stress "surge protector." According to researchers at the Mayo Clinic, exercise helps the body fight anxiety by producing endorphins, the body's natural opioids, that help produce a hormonal sense of strength, confidence, and wellbeing. Research published in the *Journal of Physiology* further found that aerobic exercise facilitates the creating of new nerve cells in the hippocampus, a brain structure that plays an important role of the processing of memory and emotion. In general, the "beefier" the hippocampus is, the more adept the person is at managing stress.

Better yet, you don't even need to work out long. According to the American College of Sports Medicine, seven minutes of a type of exercise known as "high-intensity interval training" (HIT) can yield tremendous benefits. In fact, work by researchers at McMasters University found that HIT creates molecular changes in the muscles similar to those produced by several hours of biking or running. HIT involves alternating between vigorous stimulation of the muscles of the upper body (weights, push-ups, planks, etc.) with vigorous stimulation of the lower body (squats, crunches, abductions, etc.) with a brief, more restful interval in between, usually involving light cardio. There are many different HIT programs, and you can learn more about them by consulting your physician, physical therapist, or a personal trainer. The point is, almost anyone can manage to exercise for seven minutes a day. If you are struggling with the physical effects of stress and anxiety, make sure to take a few minutes to beef up your body's anxiety-fighting potential.

NUTRITION AND SUPPLEMENTS

Also underappreciated is the role our diet and natural supplements can play in helping the body be a more effective surge protector against anxiety. According to a report compiled by the Harvard School of Medicine, food rich in magnesium (e.g., leafy greens, legumes, nuts), zinc (e.g., oysters, cashews, liver, beef, and egg yolks), probiotics (e.g., sauerkraut, pickles, yogurt), and B vitamins (e.g., avocados, almonds, etc.) all help the body fight anxiety. These foods increase the production of neurotransmitters such as serotonin, which counteracts the effect of stress on the nervous-system, and dopamine, which produces "feel good" sensations and a sense of accomplishment. As with sleep, a less anxious person may be able to function acceptably well with poorer nutrition, but the more stressed and anxious we are, the more we need to eat foods that enhance our body's stress-diffusing power.

In addition to food, various nutritional supplements have been shown in randomized, double-blind, placebo-controlled studies (the "medical gold standard") to be effective in the body's fight against anxiety. Valerian root, Rhodiola, lemon balm, passionflower, kava kava, ginkgo biloba, and chamomile are all recommended by the American Psychiatric Association's Task Force on Complementary and Integrative Medicine as both effective and safe supplemental treatments for anxiety. Likewise, the journal *Phytomedicine* published a multi-center, randomized, double-blind study comparing the effectiveness of the lavender oil capsule Silexan with the prescription anti-anxiety drug Lorazepam (brand name, Ativan). Researchers found that Silexan was as effective as Lorazepam for fighting anxiety, with the added benefits of having no sedative-related side effects and no risk of dependence, both of which can be a serious concern with anti-anxiety medications. Consult your physician to determine which supplements will work best for you.

Food scientists tell us that food and supplements should be thought of as drugs that not only nourish the body but impact the body for good or ill. God has provided a wonderful bounty for us, and eating responsibly and using natural treatments where possible is a terrific first line of defense against anxiety. Maintaining good nutrition and using supplements that have empirical support for their anxiety-fighting properties can be incredibly effective ways to help your body fulfill its role as a stress surge-protector.

MEDICATION AND THERAPY

Medication is a surprisingly controversial option for treating anxiety. Broadly speaking, anxiety-fighting drugs fall into two categories; anti-depressants (SSRIs, SNRIs, and tri-cyclic antidepressants) that do double duty as anti-anxiety drugs by helping the brain manage stress in general and drugs that specifically focus on calming a person down (benzodiazepines).

Most doctors and lay people believe that medication combined with therapy offers the best results for treating anxiety, but the most recent research disputes this assumption. According to researchers at the University of Manchester and the Norwegian University of Science and Technology, who completed the most comprehensive research project to date examining anxiety treatments, psychotherapy alone (specifically, a type called cognitive behavior therapy or CBT) was actually the most effective method of treatment, beating both medication-alone and combined therapy/medication approaches hands-down.

The research showed that while medication can yield short-term benefits for anxiety sufferers, in the long term, it actually caused patients to become embedded in their anxiety. By contrast, 85 percent of patients receiving CBT alone experienced either significant relief or complete recovery from their anxiety. But why would people receiving both medication and psychotherapy have worse outcomes than people receiving CBT alone? Researchers found that patients who took medications, even if they participated in CBT, benefited less from therapy because of a tendency to lean too heavily on the medication to do the work for them. Unfortunately, medications can only do so much. Because of that people in the CBT-only group had an easier time, long-term, learning skills and making life changes that enabled them to beat anxiety and keep it away. Those in the combined medication and therapy group tended to get stuck at a lower, but persistent, level of anxiety that was more resistant to treatment over time.

This is unfortunate. Considering that 1 in 6 people in the United States are on psychiatric medications of some kind and that Xanax, a popular benzodiazepine, is the third most common psychiatric drug prescribed, it is not unreasonable to assume that many or most people taking these drugs are not receiving any kind of psychotherapy. The Anxiety and Depression Association of America estimates that less than 37 percent of anxiety sufferers receive any kind of treatment (CBT, medication, or combined) *at all*. Based on the most recent research, it would appear that even less are receiving anything like adequate treatment. The good news, of course, is that with proper treatment (i.e., CBT alone) most people will experience a full recovery from their anxiety disorders.

If you are currently on medications for your anxiety, do not make any changes without consulting your physician, but do talk to your doctor about getting a referral to a good CBT therapist and about weaning off your medications over time so that you can make a full recovery from your anxiety.

A BODY OF ANXIETY

God created our bodies to be more than a weight we drag around. He speaks to us through them, telling us, through the language of the body, what we need to do to optimize our body's ability to cooperate with God's grace and cultivate a "peace beyond all understanding" (cf. Phil 4:7). To learn more about how your body can be your best friend in the quest for peace, talk with a therapist who is trained in integrative approaches to mental health treatment and/or a physician who specializes in functional medicine. For those readers who are rightly concerned about questionable spiritual and philosophical practices that can often be associated with integrative and complementary approaches to mental health treatment, the Pastoral Solutions Institute (CatholicCounselors.com) can assist you in finding integrative approaches to treating anxiety that are consistent with our Catholic Faith.

CHAPTER SEVEN

Straighten Your
Thinking Cap

"Is my anxiety caused by a chemical imbalance? How can psychotherapy help if it is?"

My associates at the Pastoral Solutions Institute and I field this question dozens of times a week from clients who wonder to what degree psychotherapy can really help them in their fight against anxiety. It's a fair question. If anxiety is, to a large degree, caused by the various chemicals produced in the brain and the way the various structures in the brain interact with one another, how can talking and thinking differently about my problems really make that much of a difference?

The truth is, effective modern approaches to psychotherapy, such as cognitive-behavior therapy, are less like chatting with a friend and more like physical therapy for the brain. While chatting with a friend can certainly help manage mild to moderate stress (and, in fact, I highly encourage it) the techniques used by a CBT therapist have been shown by many brain-imaging studies to actually change the ways a client's brain functions. The fields of psychoneuroimmunology (the study of how the mind affects the body's health defenses) and interpersonal neurobiology (the study of how our relationships affect our brain's development and functioning) have powerfully demonstrated in multiple studies over the last twenty years that every thought we think, every choice we make, and every behavior we display sends a wash of chemicals through us that produce profound physical changes in our body and brain. Healthy thoughts, supportive relationships, and positive life choices actually optimize the production of hormones and neurotransmitters that boost our immune system, decrease our body's inflammatory response (resulting in less pain and more ease of motion), heal tissue damage, and promote rapid, efficient communication and increased neural connectivity throughout the various regions of the brain. In fact, healthy thoughts and life choices can stimulate the growth of new neural pathways and the creation of new nerve cells that allow us to learn and adapt in healthy ways to the most stressful environments.

Similar research has shown that the opposite is also true. Unhealthy thoughts, unsupportive and stressful relationships, and negative life choices create a chemical stew that depresses our immune system, increases inflammation throughout the body, damages the skin and other organs of the body, and causes the brain and nervous system to resist both learning and adaptation. The unhealthier our thinking patterns, relationships, and life choices are, the more our body produces chemicals that inhibit the growth of neural connections between different brain regions and prevent the growth of new neurons that make learning and change possible.

This should not come as a surprise to any Christian. Christianity has always taught that there can be no meaningful separation between the soul and the body. What affects one automatically affects the other, and vice-versa. Analogous to the fact that God, as Trinity, is an intimate union of Father, Son, and Holy Spirit, the human person — made in God's image and likeness — is an intimate union of body, mind/soul, and relationships.

The good news is that we now understand that healthy thinking patterns and changing destructive relationships and behaviors can actually reverse the damage done to the brain and inflicted on the body by a less healthy past. Psychotherapy, especially empirically based approaches like CBT, focuses on teaching clients psychological techniques that have been shown to help heal the physical damage that stress and trauma can do to the brain and body. In his book *The Neuroscience of Psychotherapy*, Pepperdine University psychology professor Louis Cozolino summarizes research showing that most emotional problems, like anxiety, are caused by a failure of the different major regions of the brain to work effectively as a team. Cozolino argues that psychological techniques help facilitate the top-down, left-right functioning of the brain, allowing the brain to better manage stressful situations and emotions.

When an anxious person suffers from top-down disintegration in the brain, the cortex (thinking brain) and limbic system (feeling brain) fail to work together effectively. Sometimes, the limbic system grows so powerful that it constantly floods the cortex, causing you to experience an overwhelming rush of emotion that forces you to react rather than respond to stressful events. You can observe yourself making unhealthy choices and criticize yourself for it, but you feel powerless to change your behavior. Other times the reverse is true, and the cortex is too strong to allow the limbic system to appropriately express emotion. When this happens, the thinking brain essentially plugs up the emotional "chimney" (the Hypothalamic-Pituitary-Adrenal Axis or HPA-Axis) that enables you to appropriately vent stress and, instead, drives stress down into your body. This tends to cause somatic disorders like irritable bowel syndrome, fibromyalgia, and other highly stress-related physical illnesses.

As opposed to top-down disintegration, people with left-right disintegration find that the left (more logical, analytical) and right (more emotional, global) hemispheres of their brains don't cooperate well. If the right hemisphere is stronger than the left, it might result in strong emotional reactions you struggle to understand or explain. This leaves you wrestling with confusion. "Everything seems fine! Why do I feel like this?" This disconnect can leave you feeling powerless because you can't put a finger on what could possibly be causing your anxiety.

By contrast, when the left hemisphere overwhelms the right, this may cause you to often live in denial of your emotions, believing yourself to be highly rational despite some very irrational, maladaptive ways of acting and relating. In fact, despite this type of left-right disintegration you may have very powerful emotional reactions. Unfortunately, you might be unable or reluctant to recognize the degree to which your emotions affect your decisions. This may require you to spend an immense amount of energy rationalizing foolish and even destructive choices that trap you in unhealthy, idiosyncratic ways of being and relating.

In reality, most people struggling with emotional problems, especially anxiety, experience some degree of both top-down and left-right disintegration problems. These are not hard-and-fast distinctions. But for the purposes of developing the most direct path to healing, it can be helpful to understand which cognitive skills need to be beefed up in order to have a more balanced, brain-based approach to healing.

The following quizzes can help you determine whether your anxiety is more related to a problem with Top-Down brain integration, Left-Right integration, or some combination of the two, as well as the direction (Top-

Down, Down-Up, Left-Right, Right-Left) of the particular imbalances you are experiencing.

Down-Up Dis-integration Quiz

Evaluates the tendency of input from your lower brain (limbic system) to overwhelm your higher brain (cortex).

Answer T or F

_____ I experience my emotions as a flood of feelings.
_____ I often feel carried away by my emotional reactions.
_____ People tell me I need to calm down but I just can't.
_____ I feel powerless over my emotional reactions.
_____ I often display emotional reactions that other people tell me are out of line with the situation.

Scoring: 1 point for every T answer. _____

Anxiety Theme of Down-Up Dis-integration: "I feel 'too much' all the time." Anxiety results from feeling emotionally overwhelmed and powerless over your reactions.

Top-Down Dis-integration Quiz

Evaluates the tendency of your higher brain (cortex) to shut down input of your lower brain (limbic system) and push stress back down into your body.

_____ I am not very good at identifying or expressing my needs.
_____ I keep my feelings to myself as much as I can.
_____ I don't necessarily feel stressed but I do suffer from significant, chronic problems with (give one additional point for each):

_____ Bowel problems
_____ Body aches/joint pain
_____ Headaches

_____ Immune response (either over or underactive)

_____ Alcohol or drug abuse

_____ Behavioral addictions (videogaming, pornography, gambling, work, etc.)

_____ I actively avoid conflict even when it causes me problems to do so.

_____ I don't like to ask for help. I prefer to handle things by myself.

Scoring: 1 point for every T answer. _____

Anxiety Theme of Top-Down Dis-integration: "I feel my emotions, but I work hard not to let them out." Anxiety results from repressing feelings and physical manifestations of stress.

Right-Left Dis-integration Quiz

Evaluates the tendency of your right brain (emotional/global/impressionistic) to overpower your left brain (analytical/detail-oriented/linguistic).

_____ I often have strong emotional reactions I struggle to completely understand.

_____ I have a terrible time making decisions because I feel so many conflicting emotions.

_____ I have a hard time identifying what triggers my emotional reactions.

_____ When I'm upset, I have a hard time talking myself down. I need other people to talk me through my reactions.

_____ I often feel like I'm experiencing a big jumble of emotions I struggle to sort out.

Scoring: 1 point for every T answer. _____

Anxiety Theme of Right-Left Dis-integration: "I WANT to understand my feelings, but I can't. I like talking about my feelings but I tend to go in circles when I do." Anxiety results from confusion about the source of one's feelings and the frustration of being unable to pinpoint a cause or solution.

Left-Right Dis-integration Quiz

Evaluates the tendency of your left brain to overwhelm your right brain.

_____ I consider myself to be highly rational and unemotional.
_____ People accuse me of being unemotional or not empathetic.
_____ I have a hard time relating to people who are too emotional.
_____ I think it is silly or painful to talk about feelings.
_____ When pushed to share my feelings I tend to go blank.

Scoring: 1 point for every T answer. _____

Anxiety Theme of Left-Right Dis-integration: *"I either don't have or don't like to admit having feelings." Anxiety results from denial of emotions and/or extreme avoidance of emotional issues.*

UNDERSTANDING YOUR RESULTS

The above instruments are not meant to diagnose any particular disorder. They offer a thumbnail sketch of the potential brain dysregulation issues that may be contributing to your particular experience of anxiety. Chances are, you have some elements of both Top-Down and Left-Right Integration issues. The exercise further illustrates that not everyone's experience of anxiety is caused by the same constellation of problems, and it suggests some areas you might need to develop in order to experience greater relief from your anxiety.

Depending upon the unique imbalances you are experiencing, psychological techniques in general, and psychotherapy in particular, can offer strategies to strengthen your underperforming brain regions. This helps you regain — or develop for the first time — your ability to effectively identify, manage, and appropriately express emotions, and more consciously manage the role of emotions in your life and relationship choices.

In the next few chapters, I'll provide simplified, do-it-yourself versions of three techniques that associates at Pastoral Solutions and I use to help people win the battle against anxiety. Each one is designed to help decrease your anxiety by improving both Top-Down and Left-Right functioning in your brain. All together, these exercises will help you strengthen the cognitive processes that serve as psychological surge protectors to stop anxiety from knocking you offline.

CHAPTER EIGHT

Installing a Cooling System

A COOL BRAIN IS A HAPPY BRAIN

Anyone dealing with stress, worry, or anxiety does well to remember that a cool brain is a happy brain. Your brain works incredibly well as long as there is good, bi-directional, top-down, left-right integration. The more you tend to experience disintegration between your limbic system, cortex, and left and right hemispheres, the less efficiently your brain can process stress and the more "heat" gets generated. The "hotter" your brain gets, the more you are prone to feeling stressed by your environment and emotions. In fact, you could think of stress as a sign of a brain that is running hot. In this chapter, we'll explore how you can upgrade your brain's cooling system so that it can process all the stress of this broken world and still function at its peaceful best.

The first step in our brain-cooling exercise is becoming adept at taking your mental temperature throughout the day. Most people are so concerned with the things happening to them that they don't pay much attention to the effects those events are having on them. They are consistently surprised when they suddenly feel overwhelmed, are gripped with anxiety, crushed by panic, or struck with stomach, head, or body aches. To them, these reactions feel as if they "came out of nowhere."

That is why, as underwhelming as it can sound, turning our attention inward is key to managing the outside influences of stressful situations. The more aware we are of our internal stress temperature, and the more sensitive we can become to its small fluctuations, the more effective we can be at managing it. We can learn to keep our stress temperature low enough that even in the most stressful of environments, we can keep a "cool head" about us and manage the situation in a conscious, intentional manner.

Let's imagine our stress-temperature scale running from 1 (cool) to 10 (boiling over). Our minds tend to function at their best around a 3, but this is difficult to maintain at all times. For our purposes, anything below a 7.5 is workable (but working to keep your temperature at 6.5 or lower is ideal). Let's look at each point on the stress temperature scale.

STRESS TEMPERATURE SCALE AND ANXIETY

1–2: **You are very relaxed, well-rested, and relatively attuned to what is going on around you.** At this level, you may feel a bit understimulated.

3: Flow. This is the state of perfect balance between relaxation and attention. This is the point psychologists refer to as "flow," where you feel at one with your performance. Even stressful moments are perceived as exciting opportunities. This idealized state is a peak state of being but, as such, is difficult to maintain except for short periods that can be increased with practice.

4: Contented Engagement. At this stage, while you are not quite in a state of flow, you feel competent and confident in your ability to handle your environment. You are happy to be doing what you are doing.

5: Engagement. You feel competent in your ability to handle your circumstances, but you are neither happy nor unhappy to be doing what you are doing. Instead, you are happy to be accomplishing things, if not altogether happy about the accomplishments themselves.

6: Stressed Engagement. At this point, your body begins producing a slow, steady drip of adrenaline and cortisol into your blood stream. You feel mildly stressed or harried. You are still in control of yourself and your situation but you have to concentrate to not seem irritable to the people around you. At this stage, you would prefer to not be perceived as anxious or irritable by others. You are careful to present yourself well and appear to be "keeping it together," even though you are looking forward to this time being behind you. As your stress pushes you up toward a 6.5 or closer to a 7, it gets harder to remember to be polite, civil, and solution-focused. Although you might be loath to admit that you are actually stressed or anxious, others might begin asking you, "Are you okay?" as you are starting to show more rough edges than usual.

7: Stressed. Adrenaline and cortisol are building up in your bloodstream. You are now stressed, although you may still not be willing to admit it. The non-verbal filters in your brain are under assault, and you are beginning to openly display signs of irritation, frustration, and disgust. You may be prone to roll your eyes, grimace, sigh, fidget, pace, or produce other non-verbal signs that you are getting fed up. Beyond this point, most people's brains become seriously overheated, and we lose our ability to respond intentionally to our emotions and reactions.

7.5 ------------ CUTOFF POINT ------------
Effective problem-solving is not possible for most people past this point.

8: Nervous Agitation. The adrenaline and cortisol levels are high enough that your non-verbal brain filters are now offline and your verbal filters are beginning to collapse. You may notice yourself speaking faster than your mind can keep up. You may begin complaining to yourself or lecturing or venting to those around you. You may tend to feel powerless and are strongly tempted to blame the people around you or your circumstances for being too difficult to manage. You may find that you are always busy but never getting anything done because of an inability to focus properly. This is the first stage when most people are willing to admit to themselves that they are stressed or feeling anxious, because at this point it becomes unavoidable.

Unfortunately, once your temperature is at this point, you may be too stressed to do anything except ride it out. With practice, some people can consciously bring their temperatures down at this stage, but this is an acquired skill. If you have not been practicing, chances are you do not have the ability to consciously self-regulate at this level. You will have to escape the situation (or let it pass) in order to calm down.

9: Anxiety. Your body is beginning to overdose on adrenaline and cortisol. Your verbal filters have completely collapsed and your physical filters are under attack. You may start talking in circles and/or find it difficult to focus. You feel fearful and overwhelmed. You are almost entirely focused on escaping your situation rather than figuring out how to deal with it more effectively. You just want this moment to end. You may feel your mind going blank. You may also begin suffering from physical signs of stress such as muscle tightness, body aches, feeling flushed, mild dizziness, or stomach/bowel problems. You may also be experiencing mild shortness of breath, as if you were physically exerting yourself.

10: Panic. Your physical filters are collapsing and you are experiencing a sense of panic. You can't complete sentences. You find it difficult to think. The physical symptoms described above are increasing. You may experience symptoms similar to a heart attack.

KEEPING YOUR COOL

Some people feel like they go from a 1 to a 10 in no time. Despite what it feels like, this is never true. In most cases, this means that the person is at a constant 7, and he has been at a 7 for so long, he mistakes his temperature for a 4 or 5. Because he is always just below the point of nervous agitation, the minute an unusual stressor or an unusual number of stressors hit at once, his temperature increases quickly to the point that he feels overwhelmed and out of control.

The key is learning to keep one's emotional temperature at a 6 or lower at all times. This does not necessarily mean eliminating stressors from your life, especially if that is not practical and/or doing so would cause you to feel like you are giving up on important people or situations in your life.

There are two essential aspects to learning to keep your emotional temperature at 6 or lower. The first is learning to check your baseline stress temperature throughout the day, make small adjustments in the way you pace yourself, take small breaks, reach out for help, anticipate problems, and gather resources in advance of those problems. The second is learning to anticipate and manage situations that tend to cause spikes in your temperature.

MANAGING YOUR BASELINE TEMPERATURE

Again, many people who struggle with anxiety live at an emotional 7, and they have been there so long they believe it is normal. If this describes how you feel, you will need to learn to more effectively manage your baseline temperature. Use your notebook to complete the following exercise at the following points in your day:

- When you wake up
- When you start your work day
- At lunch time
- Before the conclusion of your work day (at home or office)
- At dinner
- An hour before bed

When you complete the exercise, do not ask yourself how stressed or anxious you feel. You will tend to underestimate your stress level, since most people do not like to admit that they are stressed or anxious until they are already at a 7 or 8. Instead, use the behavioral descriptions above. It doesn't matter if you feel like you are at a 6, 7, 8, etc. If the behaviors of that level more or less describe your current behavior, assume that it is the actual level of your emotional temperature. A big part of this exercise is recalibrating your internal sense of stress to stop underestimating your anxiety level. If you feel in between two stages on the emotional temperature scale, it is always better to assume that that higher number more accurately represents your level of stress and anxiety.

Baseline Temperature Exercise

Time of Day (select one)
_____ Rising   _____ Lunch   _____ Dinner
_____ Start of Work   _____ End of Workday   _____ Bedtime

Rate your **Current Temperature** (Use the behavioral descriptions, not your subjective sense of your stress level. If between two points, choose the higher).

What was the **highest** level of stress/anxiety you have felt **since the last time you checked your temperature?**

What situation or event triggered this spike in your emotional temperature?

_____

_____

_____

_____

What was the **lowest** level of stress/anxiety you have felt **since the last time you checked your temperature?**

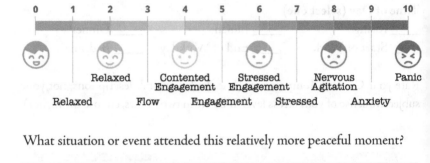

What situation or event attended this relatively more peaceful moment?

_____

_____

_____

_____

Plan: Identify one small thing you will commit to doing (whether or not you feel like it at this moment) that may allow you to make more meaningful connections with the people around you, experience God's presence in a more meaningful way, enjoy your life a little more, and/or allow yourself to adopt a calmer pace to your day.

_____

_____

_____

_____

Anticipate: By how many points do you expect this small action step will decrease your stress temperature level before your next check-in? (Write down your prediction) *1 2 3 points.*

(If you do not think an activity will lower your stress by at least 1 full point, please choose something else or add an additional stress-reducing activity.)

- **Assess:** Why do you think this small action step will decrease your stress by the number of points you indicated above?
- **Pray:** Lord, I give the next few hours of my life to you. Help me to take better care of myself, to stay connected to you and the people you have placed in my life, and to commit to those actions that would allow me to experience a greater share of the peace that you promised me. Jesus, I trust in you!

Daily Review Exercise

Now that you have several ratings under your belt, at the end of each day, review your Baseline Temperature Exercises and respond to the following questions in your notebook.

- At which rating period was your stress/anxiety the highest?
_____ Rising _____ Lunch _____ Dinner
_____ Start of Work _____ End of Workday _____ Bedtime
    - What situations attended this increase in your experience of stress/anxiety? (Who was present? What were you doing?)
    - If this stressful event occurred again, how would you want to handle it differently, assuming you felt the same way?

- At which rating period was your stress/anxiety the lowest?
_____ Rising _____ Lunch _____ Dinner
_____ Start of Work _____ End of Workday _____ Bedtime
    - What situations attended this decrease in your experience of stress/anxiety? (Who was around? What were you doing?)
    - What could you do to build more of these lower stress moments into your day tomorrow?

- What stress reducing action step lowered your stress the most today? Why do you think it was so effective?
    - How will you make time for these stress-reducing action steps tomorrow?

- How much lower would you expect your stress/anxiety level to be if you committed to making time for stress-reducing activities? (Write down your prediction) *1 2 3 points.*

• PRAY: Lord, I thank you for the gift of another day. Help me to use each day to grow closer to you and to the people I love and to cooperate more effectively with your grace that I might experience more of your peace and be more of an instrument of your peace in all things. Through Jesus Christ my Lord. Amen.

TIPS FOR SUCCESS

I understand that it might be a little tedious to do this exercise several times a day for several weeks, but I promise your commitment will be rewarded. If you do both of these exercises consistently, you will start to see a spontaneous blueprint emerge for increasing your peace in a natural and holistic way that both fits your life and makes a real difference in your outlook and emotional well-being. To get the most out of this exercise, please keep the following tips in mind.

Anticipate and plan. Keep track of the situations that give you the most stress. Learn to anticipate stress and anxiety-provoking situations, but instead of dreading them, make a plan to handle them better. What resources do you need to gather in anticipation of these stressful events? How would you like to handle them differently? Regardless of the way the situation played out, or how others conducted themselves, what would you have to do to feel proud of the way you handled yourself the next time this stressful situation arises?

Look for the differences that make a difference. Keep track of the action steps that decrease your anxiety by the greatest amount, most consistently, or both. Don't just wait for these to spontaneously occur. Make a point to build them into your day! Intentionally cooperate with God's grace.

Don't escape. Engage! Too often we think decreasing our stress requires an escape. We can't wait to give the kids to our spouse and get some "me time." We can't wait to leave work. We can't wait to escape. It's fine to want a break, but not to live for your next break. Why? Because breaks don't come often enough, and the escape never lasts. What can you do instead? Ask yourself, "How can I stop phoning in my time with these people or this situation? How can I more creatively engage this situation? How can I more meaningfully connect with these people? How can I approach this in a way that doesn't burn me out, but rather gives me energy and joy?" Anxious people tend to increase their anxiety by living for breaks and wishing their everyday life away. Then, when stressful people and situations are gone (the kids grow up, the job is lost), they bemoan the loss of that time. Everyone needs to escape once in a while (Scripture tells us even Jesus got away now and then), but we actually increase our anxiety by white-knuckling through our lives in nervous anticipation of the next break. Instead, look for ways to bring more of yourself to your experiences and relationships, not in a way that burns you out, but in a way that gives life. If you cannot figure out how to do this, you may need to seek professional assistance to help you lean into your life — or create a more meaningful life.

ONE STEP AT A TIME

In this chapter, we explored ways to cool down your brain and allow it to work more efficiently. By consistently practicing these exercises, you can stay calmer, cooler, and more collected in the middle of — not just in spite of — your life. You will discover that you no longer have to be a hapless victim of anxiety-producing circumstances. You can be a person who intentionally finds meaningful, consistent, and effective ways to manage your life. You will learn how to keep a cool head — even in the middle of the worst storms of life — and become a powerful witness to the peace God can bestow in the most anxious of hearts.

The next two chapters will help you create better bi-directional top-down, left-right integration so that you can use all the resources God has given you to lead a more peaceful life.

CHAPTER NINE

Building an Emotional Elevator

111

In chapter seven, we discussed how poor communication between your higher brain (cortex) and lower brain (limbic system), in either direction, can result in different experiences of anxiety. For instance, if impulses from your emotional, lower brain tend to overwhelm the coping resources in your higher brain, you may tend to experience anxiety as a tidal wave of emotion that takes all your resources offline. This is known as "flooding," and it is the result of a Down-Up disintegration problem.

On the other hand, if your higher brain's coping resources are too rigid and well-developed, they may tend to imprison or squash your lower brain's emotional impulses altogether. In this case, the Top-Down disintegration you experience may drive your anxiety back down into your body causing you to experience physical signs of stress rather than emotional ones.

Imagine your brain as a skyscraper. Now, imagine that there is no efficient way for the people on the lower floors to communicate with the people on the upper floors except by setting off explosions in the basement that shake the entire building. Likewise, the people on the upper floors have no way of getting the attention of the people on the lower floors except by plugging up all the sinks and toilets in an attempt to flood the basement. This would not be a very healthy building to work in!

One day, the building manager decides to build a bank of five elevators and hire a staff of messengers to carry information up and down throughout the building in an orderly fashion. This way, people in the upper floors can stop jamming up all the pipes, and people in the lower floors can stop blowing things up.

The Emotional Elevator exercise you'll learn in this chapter will help decrease your anxiety by preventing your higher brain from stuffing up all your tension and driving it back down into your body. Similarly, it will prevent your lower brain from setting off emotional explosions every time it's concerned about something. This exercise can help you safely experience your feelings and, simultaneously, find productive responses to the situations that trigger them.

The purpose of this exercise is not to decrease your immediate experience of anxiety (we'll look at that in the next exercise), but to help you find healthier ways to express your anxiety and respond to anxiety-producing events. In time, you can feel less threatened by the stressful events in your life.

Emotional Elevator Exercise

Take a page of your notebook and divide it into five columns. The columns should be labeled in the following way:

1. Trigger Event	2. Reaction	3. Internal Resources	4. Alternate Response	5. Follow-up

Each column represents an elevator that allows your brain to carry information from the higher to the lower brain (and vice-versa) about:

1. The various events that trigger your anxiety
2. The unhealthy thoughts and actions these triggers may cause
3. The resources you have available to respond in a healthier way to various problems
4. The new, creative ways you could apply those resources
5. How you can remind yourself to use these new anxiety-reducing strategies

Column 1: Trigger Event

In column one, you will identify the trigger event, that is, the event that you believe is most responsible for your anxiety. The key is to be specific and concrete. Often, when people are experiencing anxiety, they have a hard time pinning down just one trigger because they feel like four million things are making them anxious. Do your best to focus on the one, specific, concrete event that you believe is most responsible for your feelings of anxiety.

For instance, Bethany tends to second-guess herself whenever she gets together with her friends. She usually enjoys herself when she is with them, but after she leaves, she worries that she said something offensive or stupid that will make her friends think poorly of her or not want to spend time with her in the future. Here is what column one of her Top-Down Integration exercises might look like:

1. Trigger Event	2. Reaction	3. Internal Resources	4. Alternate Response	5. Follow-up
Replaying scenes from evening. Ruminating about what I said.				

In this example, the trigger is not so much the events of the evening, but rather Bethany's tendency to replay those events in her mind once she gets home. Bethany recognizes that the most immediate, concrete trigger for her anxiety is her habit of ruminating about what she might have done wrong.

Peter tends to become sick to his stomach when project deadlines for work are looming. He becomes terrified that he won't complete the work in time and shuts himself in his home office, ignoring his wife and kids until he finishes the project. Here is what column one of Peter's Top-Down Integration exercise might look like.

1. Trigger Event	2. Reaction	3. Internal Resources	4. Alternate Response	5. Follow-up
Project due in 1 week! No idea how to get this done				

Peter might feel anxious about a dozen different pieces of the project he is working on, but, upon reflection, he realized that the most stressful thing about this situation is the timeline he is working on and the fear that he just won't be able to get it done in the next seven days.

Although it might seem silly to spend time identifying the trigger, your willingness to step back, take a moment to reflect on your experience, and correctly identify the thing you are most upset about predicts your ability to solve the problem. For instance, if Bethany had just written, "I get nervous around people," she would probably feel stuck. Why? Because stated this way, the problem is too big and too broad. That description captures her overall experience, but it doesn't answer the most important questions like, "What exactly is stressful about being around people?" And "What effect does being around people have on you?" Answering those questions breaks the problem down so she can actually do something about it.

The same is true for Peter. He could have just written, "Work stresses me out." But again, this problem is too big. What exactly is anxiety-producing about work? When does he feel most anxious at work? What work situations are most stressful and what is the most stressful part of these particular events? Answering these questions allows him to pinpoint a problem and begin to identify possible solutions.

Column 2: Reactions

In the second column, write down either how you naturally tend to respond to the anxiety or what the anxiety makes you do. Here is Bethany's entry for column 2:

1. Trigger Event	2. Reaction	3. Internal Resources	4. Alternate Response	5. Follow-up
Replaying scenes from evening. Ruminating about what I said.	I try to distract myself by watching TV until I fall asleep, but my mind keeps coming back to it and keeps me awake.			

Bethany's reaction is typical of people with Down-Up disintegration problems. She floods with emotion and feels powerless, so she puts all of her energy into simply avoiding the trigger. Rather than finding a way to respond to the problem, she assumes that all she can do is ignore the situation and hope it will go away on its own. Notice, by the way, that her coping strategy not only doesn't work, it also taxes her bodily surge protectors by causing unhealthy sleep habits. This will make her anxiety worse in the long run as she becomes more exhausted and less able to manage future stressors.

Incidentally, attempting to deal with stress by using "screens" (TV, internet, smartphones) never works. Devices like these numb us as long as we are using them. But if we were to think of our brain as the ultimate smart device, taking this approach leaves the app for the stressful event open in our brain, burning up our emotional batteries. In order for an event to stop producing anxiety, we need to find a way to force-stop the app. This doesn't necessarily mean solving the problem. Often that's not possible, at least in the short term. But we can still close the mental app on an issue by identifying a short-term action-step that we believe will enable us to make some progress. Alternatively, focusing on some unrelated but still more productive use of our time (such as exercising or working on a project or using the three-step anxiety first-aid technique described in chapter two) can also be helpful. We'll talk about this more below in our discussion about column 3. Now, let's take a look at Peter's response to column 2.

1. Trigger Event	2. Reaction	3. Internal Resources	4. Alternate Response	5. Follow-up
Project due in 1 week! No idea how to get this done. Feeling sick already.	Stay in my office and work 24/7 until deadline. Make sure every detail is perfect.			

Peter's Top-Down Dysregulation causes him to force himself to ignore his needs and any other feelings besides panic. He shuts off his needs for rest and proper nutrition, connection with others, or mental breaks. Instead of allowing him to listen to his body and pace himself, Peter's higher brain drives his stress back down into his body via his HPA-Axis. This triggers his enteric nervous system, the complex neural network located in the gut, sometimes referred to as a "second brain," which aggravates his stomach and makes him feel physically ill. Like Bethany, his response to his stress actually increases his experience of anxiety over time by overloading his body's surge protectors and isolating him from social and spiritual supports.

Column 3: Internal Resources

Now that we have a clear idea of the trigger and the unhealthy ways we tend to respond, we can begin to do some problem-solving. It's time to gather some resources.

Often, when we think of resources, we imagine things outside us, like asking others for help or acquiring new skills. These can be very helpful. But what if other people aren't around? Or what if you don't have time to develop new skills? What then? Obviously, you are doomed, right? Well, fortunately, no.

The best resources are internal resources — the vast library of personal strengths, past successes, and helpful tools you have picked up along the way but may be forgetting to use in the moment. When we become anxious, the neural doors to this vast library of internal resources tend to lock down. If a library is burning down, it makes sense to seal the assets behind fireproof doors. In the same way, when our brains are stressed, our focus on immediate survival strategies causes us to ignore all the best information available to us.

Surprisingly, one of our best sets of internal resources are *virtues*. Most of us think of virtues as qualities — such as peace, patience, thoughtfulness, strength, persistence, self-discipline, self-control, etc. — that we either have or don't have. But in reality, virtues are qualities that we can build up in ourselves over time through repeated practice. A virtue is, in some ways, like a muscle that we strengthen every time we exercise it. The stronger that muscle is, the more effectively we can wield it, even in the face of difficulty or opposition. A virtue is a quality that every human being displays when we are at our best. Remember, in an earlier chapter, when I asked you to imagine your Whole, Healed, Godly, Grace-filled self? All the good qualities you imagined this version of yourself possessing are virtues.

So what? How does a list of adjectives exemplified by some imaginary vision of ourselves help us in any practical way? Because it tricks your mind into thinking that you are giving advice to someone else. Our advice to others is almost always clearer, more rational, and more solution-focused than the advice we give ourselves. According to research published in the journal *Psychological Science*, when you cultivate a virtue-based approach to problem-solving, you are able to give yourself the same kinds of healthy, objective advice you give to others.

Column 3 gives us an opportunity to think about how we behave when we function at our best — especially under pressure. We might not be very good at managing this present stressor, but chances are there are at least some times when we do better at handling our problems. This step asks us to consider the qualities or virtues we exhibit in those times that allow us to handle a situation well. It then asks us to consider what it might be like to use those qualities or virtues in this new situation.

To complete step 3, ask yourself two questions. First, "What qualities or virtues would help me be more effective in this situation if I could access them?" And second, "When I have been under pressure before, how have I displayed these qualities to some degree?"

As you reflect on these questions, remember that you don't have to believe that you have mastered patience, self-control, courage, or any other such quality. You are only looking for what virtues, objectively, you wish you could display more of.

Also, don't focus solely on the qualities that would make you "nice" or try to convince yourself that the situation shouldn't be a problem. Focus on the qualities or virtues that would help you more effectively handle the problem in front of you. Here is a partial list of some excellent problem-solving virtues and qualities that can be very useful for handling anxiety-provoking situations. Feel free to either choose from these or use this list to inspire yourself to think of other helpful problem-solving virtues.

Problem-Solving Virtues (partial list)

Courage	Humor	Wisdom	Initiative
Perseverance	Assertiveness	Balance	Responsibility
Patience	Self-control	Forbearance	Self-respect
Understanding	Love	Clarity	Empathy
Confidence	Balance	Humility	
Perspective	Faithfulness	Honesty	
Creativity	Prayerfulness	Trust	

List other useful examples in your notebook.

Again, notice that the virtues listed above are not meant to convince you to ignore or not be bothered by a problem. They are meant to help you respond to your challenges in a more intentional, less anxious way. To complete this step, ask yourself what qualities would help you manage this particular problematic situation less anxiously and where you have displayed those virtues when you were under pressure before (however imperfectly).

Here is an example of how Bethany might respond to step 3 in our exercise:

1. Trigger Event	2. Reaction	3. Internal Resources	4. Alternate Response	5. Follow-up
Replaying scenes from evening. Ruminating about what I said.	I try to distract myself by watching TV until I fall asleep, but my mind keeps coming back to it and keeps me awake.	Perspective — Like when I reminded myself to see the big picture when I was worried at work. Trust — I need to trust my friend to tell me the truth, like that time we were able to talk out a misunderstanding about her birthday.		

Bethany is reminding herself of both the qualities that would be useful in handling her social anxiety and of times she displayed these qualities. She can see that she doesn't have to pretend to be someone she is not. Bethany just has to start thinking about how she might apply these virtues she has already demonstrated elsewhere in this new situation.

Here is how Peter might respond to step 3:

1. Trigger Event	2. Reaction	3. Internal Resources	4. Alternate Response	5. Follow-up
Project due in 1 week! No idea how to get this done. Feeling sick already.	Stay in my office and work 24/7 until deadline. Make sure every detail is perfect.	Balance — Like when I planned that big event last year but still made time for my kid's play. Prayerfulness — I need to remember that God is in control. Like that time I was worried about my wife's health and prayer really kept me centered.		

Again, notice that Peter doesn't try to talk himself out of the fact that the project has to get done in time. He just looks at the qualities that would help him approach the project in a healthier way. He also finds examples of times when he displayed those qualities in a similar, though not exact, situation.

Column 4: Alternative Response
In step 4, the goal is to ask, "If I could do a good job of applying the virtues and experiences I listed in step 3, how would I approach this differently?

What *exactly* would I do?"

If you're feeling a little stuck, think back to your whole, healed, godly, grace-filled self. Imagine that your WHGG self was just as concerned about the seriousness of the situation as you are but could approach that situation both possessing the qualities you listed in column 3 and mindful of past experiences when you displayed those qualities. What would "your best self" do?

Bethany might respond to step 4 like this:

1. Trigger Event	2. Reaction	3. Internal Resources	4. Alternate Response	5. Follow-up
Replaying scenes from evening. Ruminating about what I said.	I try to distract myself by watching TV until I fall asleep, but my mind keeps coming back to it and keeps me awake.	Perspective — Like when I reminded myself to see the big picture when I was worried at work. Trust — I need to trust my friend to tell me the truth, like that time we were able to talk out a misunderstanding about her birthday.	Remind myself that my friends are honest and would tell me if there was a problem and give me a chance to work it out. If I'm still concerned next time I see them, I can ask about it, but for now, remind myself of all the ways I know my friends love and accept me.	

Here is an example of how Peter might respond to step 4:

1. Trigger Event	2. Reaction	3. Internal Resources	4. Alternate Response	5. Follow-up
Project due in 1 week! No idea how to get this done. Feeling sick already.	Stay in my office and work 24/7 until deadline. Make sure every detail is perfect.	Balance — Like when I planned that big event last year but still made time for my kid's play.	Start each day giving the situation to God in prayer. Ask him to remind me that it isn't all up to me.	
		Prayerfulness — I need to remember that God is in control. Like that time I was worried about my wife's health and prayer really kept me centered.	Work hard but still commit to family dinners, game night with the kids, and at least 15 min of daily exercise — even when I feel pressured. I do a better job when I feel like my life is balanced.	

In both examples, Bethany and Peter have developed a response that is rooted in the virtues and experiences they identified in step 3. Regardless of whether they believed they could implement the ideal response, they allowed themselves to imagine the possibility of leaning into their WHGG self instead of mindlessly following their anxiety. In the next step, we'll look at what it will take to actually remember to use these new ideas, but for now, it is enough that Bethany and Peter have begun to imagine a more intentional, virtue-based way of being.

Column 5: Follow-up

Of course, having an idea of how we'd like to handle a situation doesn't mean we'll remember to do it next time. Column 5 asks, "What support/accountability do I need to put in place to make sure I follow through with my new plan?" Some examples of support/accountability include things like the following:

+ Journaling the night before (or the morning of) to remind yourself of your plan.
+ Programming a reminder into your smartphone to pace yourself, take a break, or remember to exercise.
+ Leave discreet sticky notes in prominent places as a gentle reminder of what you want to do differently.
+ Add the intention to use this new plan to your prayer-time.
+ Give permission to someone who cares about you to offer gentle, non-nagging reminders (and coach them on what that would look like to you).
+ List other ideas in your notebook.

Notice that each of these accountability methods helps you plan the new approach before the situation actually occurs. Anyone can beat up on themselves for dropping the ball after the moment has passed. The real challenge is finding ways to remind yourself preemptively, so that your brain is primed to respond when the problem situation presents itself.

Here is how Bethany might build some accountability into her resolution:

1. Trigger Event	2. Reaction	3. Internal Resources	4. Alternate Response	5. Follow-up
Replaying scenes from evening. Ruminating about what I said.	I try to distract myself by watching TV until I fall asleep, but my mind keeps coming back to it and keeps me awake.	Perspective — Like when I reminded myself to see the big picture when I was worried at work. Trust — I need to trust my friend to tell me the truth, like that time we were able to talk out a misunderstanding about her birthday.	Remind myself that my friends are honest and would tell me if there was a problem and give me a chance to work it out. If I'm still concerned next time I see them, I can ask about it, but for now, remind myself of all the ways I know my friends love and accept me.	Before I get together with my friends next time, put a note in my smart phone calendar to write out examples of how I know I can trust them to love and accept me even when I mess up. Every day, write down one example of how other people care about me and accept me.

In this example, Bethany has created two levels of accountability. First, she has made a plan to remind herself of all the ways her friends love and accept her — and the specific times they have shown this — before she gets together with them. This way, she can go into the situation having already built up a resistance to her tendency to assume that she is socially incompetent. Second, she has created a way to remind herself every day — even on the days she is not seeing her friends — that people are, generally speaking, understanding and forgiving of any perceived flaws. The more she can become aware of this willingness of strangers or acquaintances to be kind, the more she can train her mind to expect even more understanding and acceptance from her friends.

Here is how Peter might approach the same step:

1. Trigger Event	2. Reaction	3. Internal Resources	4. Alternate Response	5. Follow-up
Project due in 1 week! No idea how to get this done. Feeling sick already.	Stay in my office and work 24/7 until deadline. Make sure every detail is perfect.	Balance — Like when I planned that big event last year but still made time for my kid's play.

Prayerfulness — I need to remember that God is in control. Like that time I was worried about my wife's health and prayer really kept me centered. | Start each day giving the situation to God in prayer. Ask him to remind me that it isn't all up to me.

Work hard but still commit to family dinners, game night with the kids, and at least 15 min of daily exercise — even when I feel pressured. I do a better job when I feel like my life is balanced. | Give my wife permission to hold me accountable to family commitments — even when I have a project due. Talk with her about how to do this so I can hear it.

Each day, write down accomplishments. Give myself credit and thank God for his grace to stay on top of things. |

Like Bethany, Peter has wisely identified both a way he can remind himself to follow his new plan when he is under pressure and a way that he can increase his sense of balance and prayerfulness every day.

RIDING THE EMOTIONAL ELEVATOR

Like with any other elevator, it isn't enough just to have one. You have to use it regularly to get any benefit. In the same way, it should be noted that the Emotional Elevator exercise is not a "one and done" type of exercise. The point is to establish a better system of communication between your higher and lower brain that allows you to make steady progress, acknowledge successes, learn from mistakes, and make concrete plans to improve future performance. Each time you encounter a specific problem — even if you have used this exercise with it before — repeat the process. You can reflect on what you did better since the last time, where you still have room for improvement, what qualities and experiences could serve as a guide for that improvement, and how you will remind yourself to take these next steps.

This exercise takes advantage of the rule of thumb that *feelings follow action*. The more you practice this exercise, applying it again and again to problematic situations until you have mastered a more intentional, efficient response, the less anxious you will be the next time. Imagine that each time you use this exercise, you create more elevator banks that connect to more floors in the skyscraper that is your brain. It is going to take some time to get all the floors connected to this new system, but it will happen. Don't give up if your anxiety persists after using this exercise once or twice. Instead, note what improvements you have made — however tiny — since the last time, and build on each small success. Intentionality is one of the best antidotes, because anxiety comes from feeling caught off-guard, unprepared, and without a plan. If you can go into a potentially anxiety-producing situation with a plan in hand, you will feel more peaceful.

Chances are, your anxiety will not all go away at once. But do this exercise each time you encounter this problem situation and make a note of any decrease in the amount of anxiety you may feel. Then take a moment to thank God for the progress you are making and give yourself credit for cooperating with his grace just a little better. Each time you use the Emotional Elevator exercise, you create new channels for grace to flow through you, bringing with it the peace beyond all understanding.

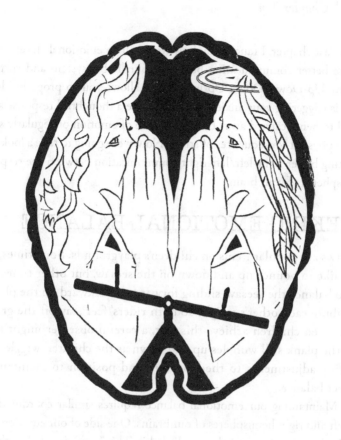

CHAPTER TEN

Balancing the Seesaw

In the last chapter, I taught you how to install an emotional elevator to facilitate better communication between your limbic system and cortex. A healthy Up-Down/Down-Up integration allows you to properly identify what is triggering your anxiety and formulate a thoughtful response as opposed to being carried away by a tidal wave of emotion or regularly struck by the physical consequences of stress. Now, we're going to take a look at facilitating better right-left/left-right communication between the respective hemispheres of your brain.

SEEKING EMOTIONAL BALANCE

Seesaws are popular items on children's playgrounds. Sometimes, children like to bounce up and down on the seesaw, but other times, they try to balance the seesaw, sliding forward or backward on the plank to distribute each other's weight so both riders' feet stay off the ground. Even when children achieve this feat, a careful observer might notice that the plank still wobbles up and down as the children wiggle, making tiny adjustments to their posture and position to maintain this perfect balance.

Maintaining our emotional balance requires similar coordination of the left and right hemispheres of our brains. One side of our emotional seesaw is always going up or down a little bit. This "wobbling" is healthy and allows us to make tiny adjustments in our internal attitudes and outward demeanor so that we can maintain the perfect balance between emotional experience and rational reflection. Maintaining this delicate balance allows us healthy levels of insight into why we are feeling what we are feeling so we can develop comprehensive responses to our situation — responses that address both the external event (the thing that's happening to us) and the internal experience (needs, memories, thoughts) that are being triggered by the external event.

Anxiety is a sign that we are "off-balance." If our left hemisphere swings up too high, we tend to run around distracting ourselves from our feelings. We complain about how busy we are, but we may fail to realize that this busyness serves a purpose. It stops us from reflecting on our internal life and acknowledging unmet needs, painful memories, or negative thoughts. In this event, our anxiety is the result of too many unacknowledged physical, emotional, relational, and/or spiritual needs that never get properly articulated, much less met.

By contrast, if our right hemisphere is on the high end of the seesaw, we tend to get stuck ruminating about our experience. We turn things over and over in our heads but feel eternally conflicted about the right answer. In this condition, anxiety tends to result because we are so focused on what's going on inside us that we can't formulate an effective response to our external circumstances. In this situation, we tend to feel powerless and trapped and may talk endlessly about our problems (both in our heads and to others) but struggle to actually do anything practical to address those problems.

This chapter's exercise is intended to help create better communication between your right and left hemispheres so that you can be aware of your internal life and respond appropriately to your external circumstances.

In chapter three, I presented a series of three questions that were intended to help you become more aware of the different layers of experience that may be contributing to psychological anxiety. The first layer was the event itself, the answer to the question, "What is happening right now?" In the simple example I used in that chapter, Karen texted Julia, but Julia did not respond to her text.

The second layer of our experience is self-talk, the internal conversation that answers the question, "What does this even mean to me or say about the kind of person that I, and other people, think I am?" Karen interpreted Julia's failure to text her back as a sign that she had annoyed Julia, and that Karen "is just a pest who drives people away."

The third layer of experience is the memories triggered by the present event. As Karen reflected on the question, "What experiences taught me to think this way (that I am a pest who drives people away)?" she became more aware of different life experiences in her past that taught her to think of herself in this negative manner.

Reflecting on these three layers of experience helps the right hemisphere of the brain to be aware of what is happening and why — on a personal level — that experience is emotionally significant. A person with left-right dysregulation issues will struggle to offer more than the most superficial answers to these questions. It will be relatively easy for her to say what happened, but she will struggle to answer the question, "What does it mean to me/say about me?" and she will be hard pressed to identify specific memories of experiences that taught her to think that way. If you struggle with this, don't give up. The struggle you experience is directly proportionate to how much you need to develop this ability to overcome your particular experience of anxiety. The struggle is not a sign that the exercise is useless or not worth your time. It is a sign that you need to exercise the right hemisphere's mental muscles a bit more in order to maintain better emotional balance.

By contrast, people with right-left dysregulation tend to find it relatively easy to answer the above questions but struggle to address a different set of questions that the left brain is more equipped to answer. These four questions are:

1. Are the thoughts and memories identified in the first three steps *consolations* or *desolations*? (We'll explore these two terms, and our use of them in terms of handling anxiety, shortly.)
2. If the thoughts are desolations, what is a healthier, more productive way to view this situation?
3. What experiences have I had to support this healthier and more productive view?
4. What action steps would this view require me to take (whether or not I feel like doing them)?

These seven questions represent the steps of the Emotional Seesaw Exercise. Here is the entire process of the exercise laid out for you. Don't worry if you don't completely understand all the steps just yet, I just want to familiarize you with the basic outline.

Emotional Seesaw Exercise

Step One: The Event

+ What is the specific event that triggered my anxiety?

Step Two: Self-Talk

+ What does this event mean to me (why/how is it significant)?
+ What does this event say about the kind of person I or others think I am?

Step Three: Memories

+ What experiences have I had that seem to justify thinking this way about myself and the event?

Step Four: Consolation/Desolation Test

+ Do the first three steps represent a consolation or a desolation?

Step Five: Attune to Consolation

+ If the thoughts are desolations, what is a healthier, more productive way to view this situation?

Step Six: Support/Resonance

+ What experiences have I had to support this healthier, more productive view?

Step Seven: Action Step/Increasing Resonance

+ What action steps could I take to help me create even deeper resonance with this view in the future?

EXPLAINING THE STEPS

Because there is a lot of information to process in this exercise and it usually takes several sessions to explain it, I broke it up into two sections in the book. We already described steps 1 to 3 in chapter three and reviewed those steps above. Let's review our example of Karen's possible answers to the first three questions:

Step One: The Event
+ What is the specific event that triggered my anxiety?
  I texted Julia and she didn't text me back. I feel really nervous about it.

Step Two: Self-Talk
+ What does this event mean to me (why/how is it significant)?
  It means that I have annoyed her.

+ What does this event say about the kind of person I or others think I am?
  It says that I am a pest that drives people away from me by being too needy.

Step Three: Memories
+ What experiences have I had that seem to justify thinking this way (see step two) about myself and the event?
  In first grade, I moved to a new school. None of the kids would play with me. When I tried to do what my mom said and ask them to do things, they just made fun of me. I spent the next three years trying not to bother people during recess so they wouldn't pick on me.

  Also, when I was a kid, my dad was very busy. He brought a lot of work home, he said, so that he could be around the family. But when I would ask him to play with me or look at a project I did, he would tell me, "Stop being such a pest. I'll look later," and chase me out of his office. He rarely remembered to follow up.

Almost everyone has experienced something similar to these simple examples. It's important to illustrate that even simple things that cause a serious amount of emotional stress do so because of the pre-conscious and unconscious memories they bring up. We are simply not bothered that much by things that don't dredge up negative memories. When something happens, our right brain processes the information more quickly and globally. It searches through the bank of our memories and says, "This (new experience) is just like that (old experience). Act like you did then." This happens very quickly, and usually it produces a sufficiently adequate response. But sometimes it goes awry.

For instance, if my friend is upset with me and says something that reminds my right brain of something my dad said or did to correct me when I was a little boy, the association created by my right brain might lead me to believe that pouting, throwing a tantrum, or walking away and pretending not to hear him could be effective responses. Obviously, this is not only *not* the case in this instance, it would be incredibly confusing to my friend. In order to change my response, I need to examine the associations my right brain is making, assess whether or not they are healthy, godly, and productive and, if not, identify both new, better associations to make and a more appropriate response. I also need to practice making these new associations and responses in order to get them to stick. This is where steps 4 to 7 of the Emotional Seesaw Exercise come in. We'll walk through these steps now.

STEP FOUR: CONSOLATION OR DESOLATION?

Do the first three steps reveal a consolation or a desolation?

In order to successfully overcome an experience that is triggering anxiety for me, I need to know whether the self-talk and memories my right brain associates with a particular experience are healthy, godly, and productive. Sometimes the answer is obvious, sometimes it's a little more complicated. For those more complicated times, we turn to Saint Ignatius of Loyola for some guidance.

Saint Ignatius developed a system for what he referred to as the "discernment of spirits." He argued that the various "movements of the spirit" we experience (which can manifest in our lives as drives, feelings, impulses, motivations) are the result of either the Holy Spirit or an evil spirit whispering in our spiritual "ear." These spirits cannot make us do anything. They can only suggest. We must choose to act.

Movements of the spirit that enable us to experience more of God's grace and love and enable us to become more of the person God wants us to be are "consolations." Consolations represent the loving counsel of the Holy Spirit that draws us into deeper communion with God and helps us make choices that are consistent with becoming the whole, healed, godly, grace-filled person we are meant to be.

By contrast, desolations represent the counsel of an evil spirit attempting to pull us away from God or throwing up roadblocks to us cooperating with God's grace to become the whole, healed, godly, grace-filled people we are meant to be.

It is important to note that there's a difference between consolation/desolation and our emotions. Our emotions can offer us important clues as to what's going on in our souls, but they do not determine our spiritual reality. For instance, feeling anxious does not necessarily mean I am far away from God. In fact, in certain instances anxious feelings, though unpleasant, could be consolations, because they are pointing me back toward God and away from some evil that's keeping me from him. At the same time, feeling great could be a desolation because I'm stuck in some sinful habit that's drawing me away from God, but I'm not motivated to change that habit and start moving toward God again because I feel good. It's important to be tuned in to the promptings we receive so that we can respond in a way that will ultimately bring us peace.

Tuning in to consolation and desolation allows us to recognize where our thoughts are coming from. We often take our thoughts for granted as coming just from ourselves, but this is very often not true. It's important to recognize when the Holy Spirit is trying to tell us something — and also when an evil spirit is whispering lies in our spiritual ear.

Building upon Saint Ignatius' model, I argue that, drawing from other teachings both in our Christian tradition and in research in positive psychology (a branch of psychology that studies the habits and thinking patterns of emotionally healthy, happy people) can further clarify what consolations and desolations look like. Specifically, consolations always point us toward meaningfulness, intimacy, and virtue. On the other hand, desolations always point us to powerlessness, isolation, and self-pity or self-indulgence. Let me explain where I am getting these distinctions.

Consolation moves us toward *meaningfulness* by leading us to use our gifts and talents to make a positive difference. We tend to feel that our life is meaningful if we feel we have "made a difference" in some way. In both big and small matters, consolation always nudges us to make the most meaningful response possible in a particular situation. A great deal of research in positive psychology points to the importance of meaningfulness, the ability to use our strengths, gifts, and talents to have a positive effect on both the people around us and the circumstances in which we find ourselves (Seligman, Martin. *Authentic Happiness*. New York: Atria Books, 2004). Meaningfulness is akin to the term "self-donation," which Saint John Paul II wrote about in his *Theology of the Body*. The Church teaches us that it is by making a gift of ourselves (cf. *Gaudium et Spes* #24) — which includes using our God-given talents and abilities to make a positive difference in the world — that we find fulfillment in Christ.

Desolation, on the other hand, points us away from meaningfulness toward *powerlessness* by convincing us that we have no gifts to bring to the table and no ability to effect any change. *There is nothing I can do, so why bother trying?* This kind of powerless thinking separates us from our gifts and blinds us from even the tiny steps we could take to cooperate with God's grace. These kinds of thoughts stand in stark contrast to Scripture, which tells us that we can do all things through Christ who strengthens us (cf. Phil 4:13). As such, desolations lock us in a state of anxiety by saddling us with the overwhelming sense that "Things must change" while simultaneously convincing us that "There is nothing I can do."

Let me offer a brief illustration of this in practice. If I was nervous about taking on a new responsibility that I prayerfully believed would, in theory, be good for me, I *could* "resolve" my anxiety by walking away from the opportunity saying, "Sure, it would be good, but it's just not me." Yet, that response would not be as *meaningful* as figuring out how to slowly get more comfortable applying my gifts and talents in this new way. In fact, avoiding this good thing would confirm me in a sense of powerlessness. Even though sticking with the good thing and learning how to work through my anxiety to take it on would be difficult, choosing to do so would represent that I am listening to the consolations of the Holy Spirit and cooperating with God's grace more effectively. Because of this, the more I worked on meaningfully engaging this new situation, the more my anxiety would decrease with time, as God worked to heal me through this new experience. On the other hand, refusing to take on this thing that I prayerfully believe would be good for me means I have chosen to listen to the desolation that told me that I was too powerless to be truly up to the task. I would therefore remain stuck in my anxiety, convinced that because I felt anxious, there was nothing else I could do to effect positive change in my life.

The second quality that consolations will always point toward is *intimacy*. Research in positive psychology points out that happy, peaceful people work hard to make their relationships as strong and healthy as they reasonably can (Seligman, 2004). Our Catholic tradition agrees that strong, healthy, intimate relationships are a critical part of living a healthy, abundant life. God did not create us to be alone (cf. Gen 2:18). A major theme of Saint John Paul II's *Theology of the Body* is that, from the very beginning, God created us for communion. In fact, our job as Christians is to spend this life developing our capacity for intimate relationships with others so we can spend eternity in joyful union with God and the entire communion of saints. In preparation for this heavenly destiny, the Holy Spirit will always whisper consolations in our heart that encourage us to choose to make our relationships healthier and, where it is safe to do so, deeper.

By contrast, desolations from an evil spirit always push us to choose *isolation*. Sometimes this means avoiding people altogether (especially if these people would be the source of good, godly, and healthy support). Other times it means putting up with unjust treatment in unhealthy relationships that make us feel isolated even though we are surrounded by people.

The final quality consolation points us toward is *virtue*. Many people think being virtuous is the equivalent of being nice, of not rocking the boat.

That isn't true at all. Virtue is strength. Virtues are the dispositions that help us to use whatever life throws at us as an opportunity for personal, relational, and spiritual growth. Even though positive psychology is not at all religious, a great deal of positive psychological research highlights the fact that authentically happy, healthy people work hard to use all the circumstances of their life to cultivate virtue (Peterson, Christopher, and Martin Seligman. *Character Strengths and Virtues*. APA/Oxford University Press, 2004). Of course, our Christian tradition is also deeply concerned with the cultivation of virtue. Consolations always challenge us to take whatever we are going through and use it to become the whole, healed, godly, grace-filled people God wants us to be.

Desolations, on the other hand, lead us to *self-pity and self-indulgence*. Rather than seeing the good and bad circumstances of life as invitations to grow and become stronger, better people, desolations convince us that life is just a series of things that we have to get through. When things go badly or get hard, desolations tell us that the only appropriate response is to remain stuck in a place of perpetual self-pity. Alternatively, we could also indulge in self-destructive, sinful habits to make ourselves feel better in the face of hardships.

Step Four in the seesaw exercise asks us to consider whether the thoughts and memories identified in the first three steps are consolations or desolations. Do they inspire us to respond to the current situation in a manner that reflects our active pursuit of meaningfulness, intimacy, and virtue? Or do they inspire us to respond in a manner that confirms us in our powerlessness, isolation, self-pity, and self-indulgence?

As noted above, you might feel anxious whether you are listening to consolations or desolations. At this stage of the process, you are not attempting to alleviate the anxiety. You are simply trying to discern how God wants you to respond to the anxiety you are feeling. Are you feeling anxious as a response to an immediate and present danger to your physical, emotional, relational, or spiritual wellbeing and growth? In such a case, your anxiety is revealing something you should avoid, so the anxiety is actually a consolation. On the other hand, you might feel anxious about something that could potentially lead you to experience greater meaningfulness, intimacy, and virtue in your life. In this case, the impetus to avoid the situation or thing could be a desolation. Would doing whatever you feel like doing in this situation mire you in an even deeper sense of powerlessness, isolation, self-pity, or self-indulgence? If so, the impulse is a desolation and a counsel from an evil spirit.

The more we listen to the consolations of the Holy Spirit urging us toward meaningful, intimate, and virtuous action, the more we are delivered from our anxiety as our lives become more abundant and fulfilling. The more we act on desolations that urge us toward powerlessness, isolation, self-pity, and self-indulgence, the more our anxiety grows as we feel suffocated by the smaller and smaller life we create for ourselves — doing less, relating less, and trying to feel less by numbing ourselves more.

Cognitive distortions

In addition to the Meaningfulness, Intimacy, and Virtue test, cognitive-behavioral therapists have identified fifteen unhealthy thinking habits called cognitive distortions. The degree to which these cognitive distortions are present in our self-talk tends to be the degree to which we experience emotional distress. Some examples of these distortions that relate most to anxiety include the following:

Filtering (Selective-Abstraction) — Paying attention only to information that confirms my anxiety and ignoring information that could help me feel more confident. For instance, a student who has severe test anxiety, and says it is only "luck" that she almost always gets A's and B's, creates anxious self-talk by filtering out all the evidence of her competence.

Polarized Thinking — Seeing everything in terms of success or failure, instead of recognizing that everything involves a learning curve and giving myself credit for steady improvement. For instance, I didn't perform perfectly the first time I was learning a new task, so I beat myself up the rest of the day for being an incompetent idiot who is probably going to get fired.

Overgeneralization — Tending to take one situation and generalize it to every part of my life. For instance, a person who has been unsuccessful once in an attempt to make a change in his life, rather than seeking new tools, support, or resources, decides that it is impossible ever to successfully make any changes at all.

Catastrophizing — Tending to assume that the worst is always just around the corner and that even the tiniest bad thing that happens is a harbinger of disasters to come. The person who catastrophizes lives in a perpetual state of *"But what if? What if?"*

Personalizing — Tending to assume that everything is my fault or my responsibility, whether or not it really is.

Internal Control Fallacy — Believing that it is my job to make everyone around me happy. If someone is unhappy, whether or not it rightfully has anything to do with me, I MUST make them feel better or I have failed as a person.

Emotional Reasoning — Believing that feelings are facts. If I feel anxious about doing something (even if it is something that would be good for me to do), I must avoid it *because* it makes me feel anxious (and, therefore, must be bad).

Mind Reading — Believing that I can divine what people are thinking (and it's usually something bad about me). Even when they tell me what they are really thinking, I dismiss it because *I* know what they are *really, really* thinking.

There are other cognitive distortions, but these are the most common ones affecting people with anxiety. Note that each of these thoughts is a particular type of desolation (to use Saint Ignatius' term), because each one makes it more difficult to draw near to God or to cooperate with his grace. These thoughts make it harder to pursue meaningful, intimate, and virtuous responses to our problems and, instead, keep us locked in a place of powerlessness, isolation, self-pity, and/or self-indulgence. Think of these distortions as specific examples of the types of lies Satan whispers in our spiritual ear, attempting to persuade us to view things in a way that separates us from God's grace and our best selves.

This is not to say that desolations/distortions are sinful. They are just there. We do not choose to have them or act in accordance with them. But we can think of them as temptations to make unhealthy, destructive, or even sinful choices that keep us trapped in anxious ways of thinking, living, and relating.

So, let's put this into practice using our simple example of Karen and Julia. In step four, Karen must ask herself, "Does telling myself that I am a pest who drives people away from me represent a consolation or a desolation? Does my self-talk and the particular memories being brought to mind lead me to make a meaningful, intimate, and virtuous response to the fact that Julia didn't respond to my text? Or does it cause me to feel powerless, isolated, self-pitying and self-indulgent?"

It seems clear that Karen is experiencing a sense of powerlessness, isolation, self-pity, and self-indulgence in the face of this situation with Julia. In fact, the specific desolation Karen is experiencing is *overgeneralization*. She can be confident, then, that her anxiety is a *desolation* that she must work through in order to figure out how God wants her to respond to Julia and use this situation to heal Karen of her social anxiety.

STEP FIVE: ATTUNE TO CONSOLATION

Because Karen is in a state of desolation, she must now prayerfully reflect: "What is the consolation the Holy Spirit is whispering in my heart to counter the desolation I am in?" Another question she might ask is, "How could I view this situation in a way that would lead to a more meaningful, intimate, and virtuous response on my part?" Reflecting on these questions allows Karen to tune her spiritual and emotional antenna to more graceful frequency. The answers to these questions might not immediately alleviate the anxiety she feels in this moment, but as she makes healthier choices, she will experience less and less anxiety in future situations like this.

As Karen reflects on these questions, she may answer them in the following way:

> *Even though Julia's failure to respond makes me feel like a pest who annoys people and drives them away from me, the truth is, I don't know why Julia didn't respond. Since this is a little thing, I don't have to ask her now. If I am still concerned about this the next time I see her, I should ask if receiving these sorts*

*of texts from people bothers her. Then, instead of having to
guess, I can know the best ways to stay in touch with her.*

The above response would be meaningful, intimate, and virtuous. It
uses Karen's gifts of discernment and perspective. It considers the totality
of the situation and her relationship with Julia. It also challenges her to
exercise both self-control and focus to attend to the work God has put in
front of her instead of ignoring that work and obsessing over a perceived
faux pas.

With this response, Karen also wisely avoids the common trap of mis-
taking pep talks for consolations. For instance, Karen could have told herself, "You don't annoy people! Julia loves you! She probably didn't see your
message." While this is certainly affirming, it assumes facts not in evidence.
The truth is, Karen doesn't know why Julia didn't respond. Trying to make
up a reason — albeit a more positive one — is still the desolation/cognitive
distortion of "mind-reading." It doesn't lead to a meaningful, intimate, or virtuous response. It's just a way Karen could try to talk herself out of dealing
with a potential relationship problem (which could lead to more anxiety in
the long run). After all, maybe Karen's text *did* annoy Julia. If so, ignoring
it wouldn't be any more appropriate a response than obsessing over it. But
instead of just trying to talk herself out of her anxiety (which never works),
Karen has formulated a sane, measured response to the anxiety-provoking
situation that will allow her to address her concern in an appropriate, proportionate, and productive manner.

STEP SIX: SUPPORT/RESONANCE

In this step, you will work on allowing the consolation to resonate. Cultivating resonance is what will allow you to take down the intensity of your
anxiety in the moment and allow you to follow through with a more appropriate action.

The reason that desolations feel so "true" is that they are almost automatically attended by memories that anchor them in our real-life experience. Consolations don't feel as true, at least at first, because they just seem

like random thoughts we preach to ourselves. In order for a consolation to have resonance — and, therefore, full anxiety-fighting power — we need to connect the consolations with our own real-life experiences that "prove" to us that the consolation is a valid and legitimate way to think about and respond to a particular event. This step requires asking the question, "What experiences have I had to support the healthier and more productive view I discerned in Step Five?"

Karen might respond to this by writing something like the following:

> *There have been lots of times I thought I had offended some-one and was mistaken. In fact, I remember one time, when I first met Julia at our parish Bible study, I told a joke that fell flat. Nobody in our group laughed, and I wasn't even sure that they heard it. I drove myself crazy that week thinking that I had made a complete fool of myself and that Julia and the other people in the group wouldn't want to be around me anymore. But when I showed up for the Bible study the next week, everyone gave me a big hug and was just as happy to see me as usual. I made myself crazy for nothing. It makes much more sense to compare this most recent situation with the text to the time I told that dumb joke at the Bible study than it does to compare it to what happened to me in first grade or with my dad. None of us act like children, and unlike my dad, Julia usually seems happy to see me. I need to hold on to that.*

By anchoring the consolation in a real-life event, Karen can begin to allow the consolation to resonate. That resonance brings with it a sense of peace that begins to dispel the anxiety that she felt only moments ago.

That said, to cultivate full anxiety-dispelling resonance, Karen would, ideally, need to call to mind memories that — alone or collectively — packed more of an emotional punch than the negative experiences she had in grade school and in her family of origin. Sometimes that isn't fully possible when a person first starts using this exercise. However, the more you act on consolations instead of desolations, the more new experiences you create that allow you to increase resonance every time you recall them. Once you have either collected enough experiences or enough emotionally powerful experiences to offset the negative experiences that formerly gave resonance to your desolations, both the desolations and anxiety will dissipate.

Again, getting rid of all the anxiety the first time (or even the first dozen times) you use this exercise is not the point. Working to achieve a clearer connection to consolations and a deeper resonance with those consolations is your primary focus. However, the more you do this, the more future consolations will resonate, and the psychological and spiritual resonance you cultivate will ultimately allow God to dispel your anxiety and replace it with the peace this world cannot give.

STEP SEVEN: ACTION STEP/ INCREASING RESONANCE

For the most part, it isn't enough simply to discern the consolation and anchor that consolation in already existing experiences. As I mentioned above, to get full resonance with the consolation the Holy Spirit is whispering in your heart, you will need to create new experiences that will ultimately either outnumber or emotionally overwhelm the negative experiences your desolations are latching onto.

For this step, you will address the question, "What action steps could I take to help me create even deeper resonance with this healthier and more productive view in the future?" Karen might answer the question this way:

> *Because I don't know why Julia didn't respond to my text and whether or not she is annoyed by texts like that, I will make a point of asking her about it the next time I see her. Because it was a small thing, I won't make a big deal out of it. I will be honest and humble and simply say something like, "Julia, sometimes I worry about how I come off to people. Would you prefer not to receive silly texts from me during the week if I see*

something cute? Some people like them, but some don't. I like to share things with people, but I recognize that can sometimes be distracting. How do you feel about it?" Because I have this plan, I'm going to work really hard to focus on the things that are in front of me that I have to do instead of doing what I usually do and sit around watching TV trying to distract myself from all my crazy thoughts until I pass out on the couch. When the desolation tries to come back, I will remind myself of specific times I have felt God's love and specific times I have felt accepted by my friends despite my faults, and I will praise God for his goodness and love even if I'm having a hard time connecting with it.

By scripting out her response, Karen has spelled out several concrete action steps that will enable her to create new experiences that should lead to deeper resonance with the healthier and more productive view she is trying to cultivate. No doubt this will take some effort, but if Karen continues to practice this, it will not be long before she no longer feels anxiety in the face of a perceived *faux pas.* She will recognize that people sometimes misjudge things in social interactions but that she is still loved by God and accepted and affirmed by her true friends who know her and love her despite her imperfections. In no time at all, she will be able to create even more experiences of love and acceptance that will either outnumber or emotionally overwhelm the negative experiences that the desolations formerly latched on to.

This last step makes sure this exercise results in more than just a bunch of groundless platitudes that have no staying power. Rather, it empowers us to build a series of increasingly meaningful, intimate, and virtuous experiences that allow the consolations of the Holy Spirit to resonate even deeper, producing more peace each time we step out in faith.

Be aware, it is extremely important to write out this exercise and not simply do it in your head. Doing it in your head simply activates the right brain's tendency to ruminate and all but eliminates any positive benefit you might get from this exercise. I regularly share this insight with clients who ignore me for six months until they get so frustrated that they are ready to quit. Only then am I able to convince them to consistently write it out. Guess what? There is almost always a breakthrough in two to four weeks. Write it out. Do it conscientiously. Trust the process. If you are struggling, don't hesitate to seek out professional help. A trained cognitive-behavioral therapist can walk you through the steps of this or other similar techniques.

FURTHER EXAMPLES

Some of you might be saying, "Well, sure, this works for something silly like miscommunication over texting, but my situation is much worse!" Let's apply this exercise to a much more serious situation.

Charlie is a 35-year-old married father of two young children. He experiences consistent anxiety about his marriage. Specifically, he worries that his wife, Melinda (32) is going to cheat on him. She is an attractive woman who regularly gets compliments on her appearance, but she does not go out of her way to attract unwanted attention, and she has no interest in anyone but Charlie. Intellectually, he knows they have a strong marriage. Besides, his wife is home with their small children all day, and she couldn't cheat on him even if she wanted to — which she doesn't. He does a good job checking his jealousy and forcing himself not to be controlling by asking her to account for her time or questioning her choices or the way she dresses, but he just can't stop feeling insecure about his relationship. He has tried to talk his concerns out with Melinda, and she has done her best to reassure him, but nothing she says ever seems to help him feel better about his concerns. He decides to use the Emotional Seesaw Exercise to find greater emotional balance in his feelings about his marriage. Here are the results of his exercise.

Step One: The Event
+ What is the specific event that triggered my anxiety?
  Melinda looks beautiful. When I see her, I think of how attractive she is. I know that other men find her attractive too.

Step Two: Self-Talk

+ What does this event mean to me (why/how is it significant)?
  I love her so much. It would kill me to lose her.

+ What does this event say about the kind of person I or others think I am?
  She deserves so much better than me. So many men find her attractive. What if she finds someone who is a better man, better provider, better partner? She could have her pick of people to be with. Why would she stay with me?

Step Three: Memories

+ What experiences have I had that seem to justify thinking this way (see step two) about myself and the event?
  My dad cheated on my mom several times and my mom always knew about it. She never liked it, but she always said it was because dad "needed more than she could give him." She felt it was the sacrifice she needed to make for him to stay with her.

Step Four: Consolation/Desolation Test

+ Do the first three steps represent a consolation or a desolation?
  Definitely a desolation. Probably catastrophizing (because of all the "what if" scenarios) and emotional reasoning (because I'm acting jealous, not because she's doing anything wrong; I feel like I should be jealous, so I think that makes it "true"). These thoughts certainly feel true, but these thoughts and memories make me feel crazy. I worry all the time. I definitely feel powerless, isolated, and self-pitying. They do not empower me to take meaningful actions to strengthen my marriage, propel me to make my relationship more intimate, or challenge me to be a stronger, more grace-filled, virtuous person. They make me act as if I have already lost everything and that the only thing to do is worry and fight my tendency to be possessive and jealous.

Step Five: Attune to Consolation

+ If the thoughts are desolations, what is a healthier, more
productive way to view this situation?

*If I were trying to imagine what I could tell myself to in-
spire a meaningful, intimate, or virtuous response to my
feelings of anxiety and jealousy, I would have to tell myself
that I am not my mom and that Melinda is not my dad.
Unlike my parents, we work really hard on our marriage.
She shows me in a million ways how much she loves me,
and we work really hard to handle problems as they come
up. Plus, even though I think Melinda is more attractive
than I am, she tells me all the time about the things that she
respects and admires in me. I need to remember that she
loves me as much as I love her and that we both are happy
that we chose each other.*

Step Six: Support/Resonance

+ What experiences have I had to support this healthier
and more productive view?

*1. She regularly tells me and shows me that she finds me
attractive. She also is quick to point out that she thinks
I am romantic, thoughtful, an attentive husband, and a
thoughtful dad.*

*2. We make sure to talk through problems before they be-
come big issues. When we're having difficulties, we don't ignore them like my parents did. We would never let things
pile up until cheating seemed like a "reasonable" thing to do.*

*3. We work hard to keep up our marriage. We take time
to talk and pray daily, and we get regular time together as
a couple. It wouldn't make sense to be putting this much
energy into our relationship and then sneak around behind
each other's backs. My parents took each other for granted.
Melinda and I work hard not to.*

Step Seven: Action Step/Increasing Resonance

♦ What action steps could I take to help me create even deeper resonance with this healthier and more productive view in the future?

1. Every day, even when I'm not feeling anxious or jealous, I'm going to write down the little ways Mel shows me she loves me and the little compliments she gives me.

2. When I get nervous, I'm going to re-read the last few weeks of entries in my notebook to remind myself that she works really hard to show me she cares about me and she deserves my trust.

3. I'm going to remind myself every morning that my marriage is different than my parents' marriage and why.

4. I'm going to stop picking on myself for being jealous and anxious and, instead, ask God to heal the part of me that's afraid that I'm going to repeat the kind of marriage and family life I grew up in. I'm going to also remind myself of all the ways God is faithful to me.

5. Instead of getting caught up in my thoughts, if I do all these things and still feel anxious, I'm just going to do something that either lets Mel know I love her or makes me feel closer to her. I'm not going to bring up any of these thoughts unless all of the above fails to help me feel better. If that's the case, I'll try to figure out what specific issue triggered my concern and address that instead of going down the rabbit hole with my anxious thoughts and feelings.

6. I'm going to make sure I get a good night's sleep and exercise. I feel less anxious about my marriage when I'm rested and feel good about my appearance because I've exercised.

Notice that in step seven Charlie made a point of identifying ways he could beef up his physical, psychological, relational, and spiritual surge protectors. He recognizes, also, that the time to do these things is not in the middle of a panic attack about his marriage, but every day so that he can build up resistance to his anxiety over time. Doing this exercise is like weight-lifting. You can't start weight-lifting when you suddenly have to move a stack of two-hundred-pound boxes and need the strength. You would need to exercise far in advance of any particular challenge so that you will be ready when it comes, and you do it every day to keep building your strength.

Using the Emotional Seesaw exercise to achieve emotional balance requires the same kind of daily commitment. In subsequent writings, Charlie might improve on his action steps (identified in step seven) by noting when the particular action items are working and when they are not working as well. When they are working, he might write about how to continue to build on his successes, and when they are not working as well, he might write about other thoughts and memories he hadn't factored in before that are coming to the surface now that he is dealing with the most obvious elements of his relationship anxiety. The more he does this, the better prepared he will be, both to prevent this anxiety from occurring in the first place, and to respond to it efficiently when he does.

If Charlie finds himself struggling to follow through on any of these action items, or they aren't packing the emotional punch he is looking for after several weeks of trying, he will know that it is time to seek professional support to get new skills.

YOUR TURN

Now it's your turn. Choose a situation that triggers anxiety for you. Try to be as specific as you can. Use the information in this chapter to answer the questions under each step and identify the action steps you will take to build your psychological resistance to the anxiety you feel.

Step One: The Event
+ What is the specific event that triggered my anxiety?

Step Two: Self-Talk
+ What does this event mean to me (why/how is it significant)?

+ What does this event say about the kind of person I or others think I am?

Step Three: Memories

+ What experiences have I had that seem to justify thinking this way (see step two) about myself and the event?

Step Four: Consolation/Desolation Test

+ Do the first three steps represent a consolation or a desolation?

Step Five: Attune to Consolation

+ If the thoughts are desolations, what is a healthier, more productive way to view this situation?

Step Six: Support/Resonance

+ What experiences have I had to support this healthier and more productive view?

Step Seven: Action Step/Increasing Resonance

+ What action steps could I take to help me create even deeper resonance with this healthier and more productive view in the future?

  ❏ Physical Action Steps (Are there changes to my diet, sleep schedule, or activity level that would help me cope more effectively with this problem?)

  ❏ Psychological Action Steps (How can I remind myself to refocus on more productive ways to think about this situation, more resourceful memories, or more meaningful, intimate, or virtuous responses to this situation?

  ❏ Relational Action Steps (How can I either rely more effectively on others, set appropriate boundaries, or seek additional assistance that will help me manage this problem better?)

  ❏ Spiritual Action Steps (How can I utilize prayer, the sacraments, or other spiritual supports to help me focus on more productive ways to respond to this problem?)

Revisit your plan daily and ask the following questions.

+ What is working?
+ When am I struggling to follow through on my action steps?
+ What new complications do I need to address moving forward?
+ What new resources (skills, support) might I need to make more steady progress?

Use the Emotional Seesaw Exercise every day to process the above questions and/or overcome new threats to your success.

The following prayer can help you bring your mind to God and open your heart to the changes he wants to effect in you.

> Lord Jesus Christ, my mind is anxious and troubled, but I know that you have the answers that I am looking for. Give me the grace to make the changes in my life that will allow me to experience the peace that only you can give. Help me to reject all desolations that lead me to feel powerless, isolated, self-pitying, or self-indulgent. Teach me to listen only to the thoughts that lead me to respond in meaning-ful, intimate, and virtuous ways to the problems I face and the feelings I wrestle with. Empower me to refocus on only those experiences that remind me of your faithfulness and my strength through trial, and make up for what I lack so that I can find the strength to faithfully follow through on making those changes that will bring me to a new place of peace and contentment. Amen.

CHAPTER ELEVEN

Strengthening Your Relationship Surge Protectors, Part I

153

> *We are a single body. … Distance separates us, but love unites us,*
> *and death itself cannot divide us. — Saint John Chrysostom.*

We tend to think of our relationships as somehow separate from ourselves. Because of this, when anxiety strikes, we feel that we are all on our own, and that it is entirely up to us to deal with stressful situations and/or the resulting anxiety. This idea of "other-ness" is, to use the terms from the last chapter, a *desolation*, a lie from Satan that separates us from one of the most powerful surge protectors God has given us to protect our fear/threat system from becoming hyper-activated.

Recent studies in the field of interpersonal neurobiology, the science of how relationships impact the brain's neurological functioning, tell us that relationships are like food. They don't just affect us externally, they actually impact us on a molecular level and become part of us. For instance, structures in the brain called mirror neurons cause us to feel things that other people feel. If your child stumbles and falls, you will probably wince. Why? Because your mirror neurons altered the molecules that make up your hormones and neurotransmitters in such a way that you not only remembered what it was like to fall and hurt yourself, but you also actually had a taste of the feeling of falling and hurting yourself. By recreating the actual emotional experience inside of your body, your mirror neurons enable you to empathize with your child intellectually, physically, and emotionally. In a very real sense, because your mirror neurons replicated your child's experience of injury, that experience became a part of you on a molecular level. That's why, when you recall the event, you can feel it as if it actually happened to you.

The same is true with emotional states. Have you ever laughed only because the people around you were laughing? Have you ever felt sad, angry, agitated, or anxious, not because there was anything wrong with you, but because the people around you were struggling in some way? In each of these instances, your mirror neurons reacted to the experiences of your friends and family and stimulated the production of hormones and neurotransmitters inside of you so that you could feel what they were feeling. Their experiences literally became a part of you on a molecular level, encoded in your hippocampus, so that you could recall not only the experience, but the associated feelings.

Have you ever felt happy, sad, or tense the second a particular person walked into the room — before they even did or said anything? That's because your hippocampus, the part of your brain responsible for remembering earlier feelings, recreated the hormonal and neurological states you experienced the last time you were with this person. Your relationship with that person and the sum of your experiences of that person have become a part of you, for good or ill. Even if that person dies, and some experience brings him to mind, your hippocampus will stir up the molecules in your body so that you feel he is actually there with you, inside of you. In a sense, he is.

Remember, we discussed in chapter four how the brain is wired to emphasize negative experiences except in one condition: when we feel connected to and supported by the people around us. Relationships become a part of our neurological functioning on a molecular level. We recreate inside of us the support, neglect, or trauma we experience from others. Like a fingerprint, each of our relationships creates a swirling molecular pattern inside of us that is unique to that person and the sum of our experiences with that person.

Having good rapport with supportive people isn't just a crutch or a nice benefit. It is a significant contributor to our ability to physiologically process stress. Healthy relationships have been shown to reduce the body's inflammatory response (i.e., joint pains, achiness, swelling) and increase the body's immune response, making us more germ-resistant. The opposite is also true. Unhealthy relationships increase the body's inflammatory response and decrease the immune response. When Scripture tells us that we are "one body in Christ" (cf. Rom 12:5), it is not speaking metaphorically. In a real way, every single person in our lives becomes a part of us. The more time we spend with a person, the truer this is. There is a reason that people with fibromyalgia and irritable bowel syndrome often have histories of abuse and neglect in their families of origin and/or present relationships. The latest research suggests that, to a large degree, these diseases reflect the physiological imprint of unhealthy relationships.

Loneliness, too, has a powerful physiological impact. A study published in the journal *Cell* found that the absence of social connectedness caused a decrease in dopamine in the body. Dopamine is the "reward" neurotransmitter that gives a feeling of euphoria. Dopamine is produced when we are around other people we experience as loving and supportive. But chemicals such as drugs or alcohol, and certain rewarding experiences, also trigger dopamine production. In light of this, it should not come as a surprise that many anxious people, especially men, attempt to self-medicate their anxiety with drugs, alcohol, or compulsive behaviors. In fact, there is evidence that many addictions, whether chemical (drugs and alcohol) or behavioral (gambling, sex, work), are at least strongly influenced by the addict's attempt to artificially produce the dopamine levels most people enjoy from healthy relationships. This may be why at least six of the famous "Twelve Steps" of Alcoholics Anonymous (AA) and Narcotics Anonymous (NA) involve healing and changing relationship attitudes. Healthy relationships are a key to healing addictions because addictions are often a desperate, maladaptive response to low dopamine levels caused, at least in part, by unfulfilling, unhealthy relationships.

This is a particularly important thing to consider in the face of the current opioid epidemic. Opioids can result in the production of up to ten times the amount of dopamine produced by social interaction or sexual intercourse. Combine this fact with a study of 14,000 children by Columbia University in conjunction with the London School of Economics that found that a full 40 percent of children in the United States exhibit insecure attachment, up about 10 percent since the 1980s. You can see how the increase in the need for anxiety-busting, dopamine-increasing opioids corresponds with the decrease in secure attachment.

It should be obvious that healthy relationships play a critical part in our brain's surge-protection system. As such, the next two chapters will look at three ways to maximize the anxiety-fighting power of your relationships. First, we'll discuss how to strengthen healthy relationships and experience to a greater degree to maximize the anxiety-busting, health-promoting power of your relationships. Second, we'll look at how you can more effectively ask for and receive the help you need to manage stress and stressful situations. Finally, we'll briefly explore how to appropriately use boundaries to make unhealthy relationships both healthier and safer.

MAINTAINING HEALTHY RELATIONSHIPS

Many people treat relationships as accessories that they acquire. But relationships are actually activities that require time and energy to maintain. A spouse, a child, or a friend must be viewed as more than things that make us happy when they are around. If we deprive relationships of the priority, time, and energy they need to flourish, even the healthiest relationships will turn toxic as the people we love begin to react to our objectification of them.

Take this example. Jimmy is 38 years old and is a stock broker with a wife and three children. Because of the way international markets work, it is not unusual for Jimmy to work up to sixteen hours a day. When the market is up, he is almost euphoric. Unfortunately, when the market is down, he becomes desperate and panicked. Even though he makes a good salary, he worries constantly about paying his bills and losing his job. He reports being incredibly stressed and anxious most of the time and, in addition to his nervous anxiety, he experiences regular bouts of nausea and stomach pain.

His doctor, after ordering a number of tests that showed no physical cause for Jimmy's nausea and acute stomach, attributed the problems to stress and recommended therapy. Jimmy hated the idea of seeking professional help and tended to lean more on alcohol. Although he was not technically addicted (his body did not experience withdrawal symptoms when deprived), he was seriously dependent upon alcohol to manage his stress. He finally sought therapy when his wife and children got tired of him spending the little bit of time he had at home drinking instead of being with them. His 14-year-old son refused to speak to him after Jimmy missed yet another soccer match because he drank himself into a "nap" he couldn't wake up from. His wife warned him that he would need to choose between the bottle and his family.

"She just doesn't get it," Jimmy said in session. "I'm a mess. Work is killing me. I'm always behind and all she does is put more demands on me. I can never get a break. I have to work like this or I'm dust. Maybe I have been drinking a little too much lately, but there's nothing else that helps me turn off all the yelling in my head. I either have investors yelling at me, my boss yelling at me, or my wife and kids yelling at me. I never feel like enough. I'm anxious and sick all the time, and all my family — who are supposed to support me, by the way — can do is bust my hump that I'm not spending enough time with them. Well, I wish I could go on vacation any time I wanted, but somebody's gotta pay for their cozy lives. You gonna fix all that, Doc? Good freakin' luck!"

Jimmy's situation was on the extreme end, but it was not unique. A big part of Jimmy's treatment involved helping him learn from coworkers with more balanced lives how to set appropriate limits on his work schedule and make time for family. In fact, his boss at his small investment firm, who was fifteen years Jimmy's senior and had learned the hard way through two previous divorces, had also been concerned about Jimmy's increasingly erratic behavior. He agreed to serve as a mentor when Jimmy finally got the courage to discuss how his approach to work was eating him alive. His boss helped him see that, while Jimmy would still need to work hard to succeed, he could set appropriate boundaries at the office that let him enjoy the stress-relieving benefits of marriage and family life. As Jimmy worked to repair his relationship with his wife and kids, he found he wanted to drink less, and he enjoyed his life more. He was still stressed, but he wasn't crazed and sick with anxiety. Prioritizing his relationships helped his body and his mind relax and experience more peace.

Even if your situation is not as serious as Jimmy's, making time to strengthen your most important relationships is a critical part of decreasing your anxiety. The best and simplest way to do this is by establishing rituals of connection that safeguard your ability to effectively work, play, talk, and pray together with the people you love. Each of these things doesn't have to take more than ten to fifteen minutes a day, or forty minutes to an hour altogether. This small investment in your relationships can make a huge difference, not only in your sense of psychological wellbeing, but in your body's ability to manage stress more effectively.

Work Rituals

Simple, daily working-together rituals like setting the table, cleaning up the kitchen after dinner, tidying up the family room before bed, and other simple household chores aren't just good ways to get things done. They also foster trust, a sense that you can count on each other for help, and the feeling of "we're all in this together." If you are anxious, you probably feel like everything is up to you. Daily work rituals communicate the message that you have a community of people you can rely on for help. This is enhanced by scheduling slightly larger once-a-week times of working together to take care of the yard or engage in some other kind of household maintenance. This not only teaches children important skills related to self-efficacy (the sense that "I know how to get things done," a major stress-busting factor), but it also increases a sense of shared ownership in your home. People are less likely to make a mess they will have to help clean up, which makes you feel less stressed because there is less mess and more togetherness. Go even further and schedule a day once a month for a family service project in your parish or community. Nothing beats anxiety like being part of a team that knows how to take great care of each other and make a difference in the lives of those around you.

In your notebook, give some examples of daily and weekly work rituals as well as a monthly service project you and your loved ones could participate in to help fight against stress and anxiety.

Play Rituals

Again, a little goes a long way. Set aside ten to fifteen minutes a day to walk the dog around the block together after dinner, to play a couple hands of a favorite card game, to do a simple craft, have a joke-telling contest, or any number of other simple, creative, fun activities. A study published in the *Journal of Neuroscience* recently showed that laughing with others fights anxiety by producing endorphins, the body's natural opioid. In addition to your daily time to play together, taking time for a slightly longer weekly date with your spouse and/or a family game night reminds you that life is all about creating connection with others. Further, it deepens your confidence in the ability of the people around you to lift your spirits. Play puts the challenges of life in perspective and allows you to approach the things that make you anxious in a new, more productive frame of mind.

In your notebook, list some examples of ways you could have fun with your loved ones on a daily and weekly basis.

Talk Rituals

Make a point of talking about meaningful topics — like what was the best part of your day, what you all could do to feel closer as a family, or how you can do a better job supporting each other through a particularly challenging time — on a daily basis. This allows you to handle small issues before they become problems and problems before they become crises. Schedule regular family dinners and a weekly family meeting to talk about something a little more important than who has to be driven where and what needs to be picked up at the store. Talking is cathartic. As you learned in the chapters dealing with psychological approaches to overcoming anxiety, talking out feelings with others helps to integrate the right and left hemispheres of the brain. This helps you feel more "put together" in the face of stressful situations and enables you to form more holistic responses to the problems you encounter in both your personal and relationship life.

In your notebook, identify some simple ways you and your loved ones could make a point of talking daily and weekly about more important aspects of your feelings, life, goals, and ability to work together and support each other.

Prayer Rituals

Taking even a few minutes each day to pray with those you love about the events of your day, your desire to do an even better job caring for one another, and your openness to God's plan for your lives is a wonderful way to stand together, in God's presence, against life's challenges. Attending Mass together with loved ones, at least weekly, reminds you that you are part of God's family, and that if God is for you, no one can come against you. In your notebook, identify some simple daily and weekly prayer rituals that would allow you and those you love to join together with God's grace against the stresses and pressures of life.

****

Most people feel a little intimidated by the idea of rescheduling their lives to place marriage and family work, play, talk, and prayer rituals at the center of their plans. Resist the temptation to become anxious about this anxiety-busting strategy. Take it one step at a time and make reasonable, incremental changes. In the long-term, everything you can do to prioritize relationships with those you love will help you strengthen your social surge protectors against anxiety.

CHAPTER TWELVE

Strengthening Your Relationship Surge Protectors, Part II

Unhealthy relationships can be an incredible source of anxiety. There are, essentially, two traits that distinguish healthy, anxiety-proofing relationships from unhealthy, anxiety-producing relationships. People in anxiety-proofing relationships are committed to meeting each other's needs (willingly asking for and generously giving help to each other) and they respect each other's boundaries. In this chapter, we'll look at how you can decrease anxiety both by becoming more proficient at appropriately asking for help from others and by setting protective boundaries.

SEEKING HELP

Tally is a 32-year-old mother of two. She has a history of anxiety. She especially struggled after the birth of her second child.

"I adjusted pretty well with my first. Bill works fairly long hours, but I managed to juggle things well enough on my own. But when we had Sophie, I just felt like everything was falling apart. I was exhausted. The house was a disaster, and I just couldn't keep up. When Nathan was born, I could rest or get a few chores done when he napped. But after we had Sophie, all that went out the window. If one was napping, the other one needed attention. I couldn't even get a shower without the baby screaming for me.

"I felt like such a failure. Bill would come home and there I'd be in spit-up-covered sweats looking like somebody mugged me and near tears because I hadn't been able to do the laundry or even get dinner started. He tried not to complain, but I could just imagine him wondering what I was doing all day. I felt like I *had* to get on top of everything, but I couldn't get on top of anything and the constant sense of failure just kept whirling around in my head until I just freaked out one day. I honestly thought I was having a heart attack. I felt like my chest was tight. I couldn't catch my breath. I felt dizzy. I managed to call 911. Bill rushed home. The paramedics came and took me to the hospital. Of course, nothing was wrong. It was so embarrassing.

"Working with my therapist, I realized that I didn't think I had the right to ask for help. Honestly, I didn't really even know what my needs were. Growing up, my dad was an alcoholic, and we were all so busy tip-toeing around him trying not to upset him or add to mom's burden that we just learned to handle our own stuff, y'know? I had to learn to recognize that I had needs and not to be afraid to tell Bill — or anyone who would listen — what my needs were. It wasn't easy. It took some time to adjust for all of us. Bill was so used to me just doing everything without complaining, he sometimes struggled to take me seriously when I would tell him I needed him to pick up dinner, help more with the house, or even just take the kids and give me a break. That made me feel guilty for asking in the first place. The whole process of learning to ask for help wasn't a lot of fun. But it was either that or end up in the hospital again. We all had to learn to get over ourselves and pull together.

"I have to say, as hard as it was, it was totally worth it. Bill and I are in a much better place, the kids are happy, and I'm actually enjoying being a mom instead of feeling like a prisoner on death row. Asking for help still doesn't come easy, but I'm over the hump. It's making such a difference that I'll never go back to trying to be a super-do-it-myself mom again."

People who are prone to or struggle with anxiety often have a terrible time both acknowledging that they have needs and asking others to help them meet those needs. When our needs are unmet, we often experience anxiety. Why? Remember, anxiety represents the activation of our fear-threat system. In order for you to be healthy, your physical, emotional, spiritual, and relational needs must be met. Unfulfilled needs constitute a threat, and your brain will react to that threat.

This can be confusing because most of us think of needs as the basic things we need to function, like food, shelter, and physical safety. But what constitutes a need is really much broader and more generous. Homeostasis is the scientific term for the state in which an organism is meeting all the needs that enable it to function at its best — not minimally, but optimally. When our physical, emotional, relational, and spiritual needs are met and our various systems are functioning at their best, we have achieved homeostasis. The closer we are to homeostasis, the greater our sense of peace and wellbeing. The further we are from homeostasis, the more our brains perceive that we are under threat, and the more anxiety warns us to respond to this deficit.

Let me state this again. Neurologically, our brains are hard-wired to perceive sub-optimal functioning in our body, mind, soul, and relationships as a threat. Initially, we experience minor threats as stress, but as more needs go unmet, and our day-to-day functioning diverges more and more from optimal functioning, the more anxious we become.

Sometimes we become so used to sub-optimal functioning that we don't even recognize the constant state of threat. Our conscious minds try to dismiss it. But our lower brain, the limbic system responsible for monitoring our overall wellbeing, is paying very close attention. Our insular cortex recognizes that the various physical, emotional, spiritual, and relational systems of our body are not functioning at their best and warns the amygdala of the threat. The amygdala — the body's fire-alarm — rings louder and louder in a warning to correct the deficit and restore maximum wellbeing.

If we ignore this alarm, our anxiety becomes a part of us — a constant, low-level feeling of dread triggered by the collection of perpetually unmet needs. Unfortunately, we often can't put our finger on exactly why we feel anxious, because we have discounted all the reasons. We tell ourselves those needs couldn't possibly be the reason we are anxious! We should just suck it up and get on with it.

This ties directly in to our ability to draw strength and support from our relationships. Anxious people often see themselves as highly competent and self-reliant — either because they want to be or because they feel they have to be because no one around them will do anything. These folks tend to be accomplished masters of denying their needs and refusing to ask others for help. Anxious people have often taught themselves or been taught to treat the very impulse to seek help as selfish. But ironically, this kind of denial is actually the sin of pride!

As I point out in my book *Broken Gods: Hope, Healing, and the Seven Longings of the Human Heart*, the Church has always viewed pride as the sin of inordinate self-reliance. The sin of pride causes us to deny our inherent dependence on God and others. It makes us instead want to push through the challenges and trials of life on our own power. Pride says, "I need no one but myself, and I will rely on no one but myself." It is the deadliest of the deadly sins because it makes us obstinately resistant to the help God wishes to provide for us, especially through the people he has placed in our lives. Pride allows Satan to fill our heads with desolations about how we "need to get everything done because no one else is going to do it" and "What's the point of asking for help? By the time I explain what I need, I could have done it myself. Besides, I don't want to be a bother, and everyone is too busy anyway."

Humility, the antidote to pride, is the acknowledgment that I cannot do anything on my own — I need God and others. Only when I reach out for help can I participate fully in the Body of Christ and receive everything I need to become the peaceful, graceful, confident, and courageous person God created me to be. God wants us to ask for help. He made us to require help. Human beings are social beings. From an anthropological standpoint, that doesn't just mean we like hanging out with other people. It means that we are biologically, psychologically, and spiritually dependent upon others both for our survival and for ultimate flourishing.

Asking for help is an art. It involves several steps:

1. Reflect and discern
2. Don't treat resistance as refusal
3. Negotiate, don't capitulate

Let's briefly look at each of these steps.

REFLECT AND DISCERN

We can't ask for help if we don't know what we need. Many anxious people never think to stop and ask what they need. They just see an endless task list and push themselves until they drop. It never occurs to them that God is speaking to them through their bodies; that feeling tired is really the voice of God saying, "I want you to rest now." Similarly, a feeling of resentment means, "You're running on fumes, it's time to ask for help." Feeling stressed means, "It's better to pace yourself than to get everything done." Through it all, God calls out through our bodies saying, "I know there's a lot to do, but I love you more than all the chores you have to finish. Please take care of yourself."

Back in chapter eight, we reviewed the emotional temperature scale. I pointed out that 7.5 is the cut-off point and that over this level, our brains overheat and go into fight/flight/freeze mode. The feeling that "I have to get everything done but I can't get everything done but what am I going to do because it all has to get done!" is a fairly good sign that you are spiking to at least an 8. Use the emotional temperature exercise as described in chapter eight to keep your temperature at a 6.5 or lower. When you pause to take your temperature, ask yourself four simple questions:

1. How do I feel right now? ("What is my emotional temperature?")
2. How would I like to feel? ("What could I reasonably take my temperature down to right now?")
3. What is one small — even tiny — step I could take right now to nudge myself toward how I would like to feel?
4. Whether I want to ask or not — and whether I think they can do it or not — what do I wish others could do for me?

Questions 1 and 2 allow you to identify how you are functioning right now and how far you are from functioning at your best. Question 3 represents the small things you can do in the moment to manage your emotional temperature on the fly and bring yourself a little bit closer to functioning optimally. Perhaps you need to take a moment to pray, or pace yourself better, or put on some music, or just go to the bathroom to clear your head for a moment, or ... whatever. You aren't looking for the one big thing you can do to experience complete peace. You are looking for tiny things to do throughout the day to keep your temperature in the optimal range.

A caller to *More2Life*, the radio show my wife and I co-host, said that she was beginning to have both panic attacks and a resurgence of an old eating disorder because of stress related to working full-time and being a full-time student. When she was a teenager, she learned that the best way to manage her stress was to get a lot of alone time to clear her head. But now that she was working full-time and going to school, she didn't have any down time. Everything was falling apart. I suggested that, in addition to reconnecting with her therapist, which she was already doing, the key to her recovery was recognizing that "getting away" isn't the only way to de-stress. I pointed out that while getting alone time was wonderful, most people who manage anxiety well learn to adjust their emotional temperature on the fly. They don't wait for the weekend or vacation to de-stress. They make tiny course corrections throughout the day to keep their emotional temperature in check.

Several weeks after the show, I got a Facebook message from that caller. She wrote,

> Dear Dr. Greg and Lisa,
>
> Thank you so much for taking my call several weeks ago. It might sound silly, but it never occurred to me that I could calm myself and manage my emotions in the present without having to retreat to a quiet, lonely place. I'm working with my counselor to identify different ways to catch myself when I'm getting stressed and take small steps to take better care of myself, but I have to tell you, ever since we talked, I've been feeling so much better. Your advice gave me the necessary hope and strength I needed to continue my search for healing and peace.

Obviously, we didn't "cure" this young woman in a five-minute phone call. She had a long road ahead. But her story powerfully illustrates how the simple act of reflecting and giving oneself permission to make little changes throughout the day can make a huge difference in your overall mental health — even when you are dealing with serious levels of anxiety.

Finally, Question 4 above challenges the anxious person to stop giving in to pride. The goal of that question is to allow you to turn off the desolations that say, "I don't have a right/it would be wrong somehow to ask for help and besides there's nothing anyone can do/no one really wants to help me anyway." This particular desolation stops us from considering the possibility of seeking support from the people God has placed in our lives to support us. The question challenges us to believe that help from others should be necessary, natural, and expected, because that is exactly how God made us to function. Inevitably, people who live as lone wolves — either by accident or choice — become anxious wolves. We must challenge ourselves to find some way to let others in and let them help — even if it is more difficult, less convenient, or less efficient.

DON'T TREAT RESISTANCE AS REFUSAL

One of the most common objections I receive from anxious people to the idea of asking others for help is, "I do ask, but [name] just rolls his/her eyes and sighs, or worse, when I ask him/her for anything. I don't want people to help me if they don't want to help."

This is entirely the wrong way to look at another's resistance. First, we have to check our tendency to personalize. Often, the reason other people express frustration or irritation when we ask them for help isn't because they don't want to help us or don't love us. Rather, it is because they already have a mental plan for the next few minutes, hours, or days, and our request requires them to alter that plan. Altering any plan is a little jarring and often results in a person expressing some minor sign of frustration unrelated to their overall willingness to help or their love for you. In fact, it is their willingness to help despite the frustration of adjusting a plan that demonstrates their love for you and their commitment to work for your good. Don't let someone off the hook for helping just because they don't jump up and down the second you ask them for help. Give people the freedom of expressing a negative reaction without it necessarily being a rejection of you or your needs.

Second, even if they really didn't want to help you, that's not the point. As Christians, we don't always get to do exactly what we want, the way we want it, when we want it. We are called to do what is good. Is it good to help others even if, sometimes, we don't feel like it? Of course it is! As the Church teaches, we find ourselves by making a gift of ourselves. Not only is it unselfish to ask for help (even when other people would prefer we didn't), but it is natural and necessary to expect others to help us (even if they don't care to). In fact, loving someone means working for their good, and generally speaking, it is good for human beings to be generous to each other. That is why one of the most loving things we can do is expect that the people around us should overcome their sinful resistance to helping us in whatever reasonable way they can. Let me state that again. As Christians, it is loving to expect that the people who claim to love us will help us, and it is unloving (and potentially sinful) for us to let them off the hook for doing so. In the words of Saint John Chrysostom, "He who is not angry, whereas he has cause to be, sins. For unreasonable patience is the hotbed of many vices, it fosters negligence, and incites not only the wicked but the good to do wrong."

We sin by pride if we say, "I don't need others," or, "I don't want to need others," even if we think we have a good reason. By contrast, humility is the virtue of admitting, "I need others, and I must open myself up to the help of others even when it is hard." Anxiety is often the poisoned fruit of the tree of being overly self-reliant. Whether I choose to be that way or feel forced to be that way is entirely beside the point. We were not made to be alone. The antidote to this anxiety of isolation is rediscovering our God-given right to ask for help and expect others to respond positively to our requests for help. But how do we practice this fine art of asking for help?

NEGOTIATE, DON'T CAPITULATE

At this point in the discussion, many clients express the concern that expecting others to help — especially if they are reluctant or don't want to — is somehow selfish. Much of this impulse comes from being socialized in the false gospel of self-reliance, which I've already addressed above, but there is one other consideration worth addressing.

It certainly is possible to be selfishly demanding. We all know people who are "takers" and have no problem using the people around them, making unreasonable demands, and becoming incensed when someone dares to set a boundary. Obviously, this isn't consistent with the life of a Christian.

Likewise, sometimes other people try to make us feel selfish by telling us that what we need is stupid, foolish, or unreasonable — even if it isn't. In the face of such opposition, we often feel selfish asserting our needs. We capitulate to the pressure and pretend we don't *really* need the thing after all, which then causes us to feel anxious because our wellbeing is threatened by unmet needs. Obviously, this is an unhealthy way to live.

So, how do we know whether we are being rightfully assertive or obstinately selfish? Essentially, it comes down to your willingness to negotiate the *how* and the *when*, but not the *what*. In other words, if you have a need (defined as anything that facilitates the optimal functioning of your body, mind, spirit, or relationships), then you have a God-given right to expect that need will be met. But, you have an equally important God-given responsibility to the people around you to be flexible about the how — the means you expect to use to meet your need — and the when — the timetable on which you expect the need to be met.

Rightfully assertive people refuse to negotiate the what because they know that the things their body, mind, spirit, and relationships need to flourish have been determined by God, and attempting to faithfully meet those needs is a duty they owe to God. God delights in the flourishing of his creation. Rightfully assertive people are equally willing to discuss all the various ways their needs could be met and be flexible about the timetable, as long it reflects a serious effort to meet the need.

Perhaps, for instance, you need help with getting the house in order. You are not going to be flexible about that. You are not going to try to do it all by yourself. You have determined that you need help. You recognize that you are unable to get it all done by yourself in a reasonable amount of time. That's a healthy thing to recognize about yourself, and it is reasonable to ask me to help you figure out what to do about it.

But despite your unwillingness to be talked into attempting to do it all by yourself, you should be willing to negotiate the specific jobs you might like help with, and whether you need my help, specifically, or if we could hire someone to help. Likewise, where you might prefer to get the chores done on Wednesday evening, you would need to respect that your plan might not work for my schedule. If I weren't available on Wednesday, perhaps you would be open to my suggestion to work together on Saturday morning instead (assuming that worked for both of us).

As you can see, in this simple example, you aren't asking my permission to address "what" you need. If I try to tell you how silly you are for wanting X, you could reasonably and respectfully push back and insist that you're not open to discussing that. But, with the same breath, you could let me know that you are more than willing to negotiate *how* and *when* we get it done (as long as that represents a serious, honest, effort to actually meet the need rather than a stall tactic). People who are good at handling stress use this strategy all the time for little and big things. It's their ability to negotiate the *how* and the *when* but not the *what* that enables them to appropriately pace themselves, seek help when necessary, and still get all their needs met so that they can function at peak performance despite their stress.

By contrast, selfish people refuse to negotiate the how, the when, *or* the what. They want what they want exactly when and how they want it. Any attempt to propose alternative options is seen as an attack, a rejection, or an attempt to get control over them. This approach to help-seeking is selfish because it shows complete disregard for others' needs. "I don't care about your other obligations, responsibilities, or needs! If you loved me, you would do X, you would do it my way, and you would do it now!" This approach is truly selfish. No Christian should ever attempt to meet their needs this way, but this represents an entirely different perspective from the more righteously assertive position I described above.

At this point, some people will ask, "But what if someone wants a what that is completely ridiculous?" Often a seemingly ridiculous what is really a how or when in disguise. For instance, let's say you demand a million dollars. Obviously, this is a silly example; that isn't a reasonable thing to ask me to give you, and it isn't reasonable for you to get upset if I refuse to give it to you. But as silly as this example is, how could I respond? By asking what getting that million dollars would do for you. "If you got X, how, specifically, do you imagine your life would be different/better?"

Chances are, in this example, you might say, "I just want to stop worrying about money all the time." This statement represents the *real* need (the what). "I want to feel financially secure but the only way I can imagine that would be possible is getting someone else to give me a fortune." Now that I know *what* you really want, I could affirm the validity of your need (the what) but then talk with you about other means (the how) to establish financial security. For instance, I could help you develop a budget and a savings plan.

People don't tend to want stupid things. Sometimes we pursue good things in a stupid, inefficient, selfish, or even self-destructive way, but our actual needs are quite reasonable. If you ever feel like your needs are somehow ridiculous, don't feed your anxiety by trying to tell yourself that it's "stupid" or "wrong" to want X. Remember, your brain perceives unmet needs as a threat to optimal functioning, which triggers at least a low-level anxious response.

Instead, when dealing with a seemingly silly, unattainable, or inappropriate/immoral "need," ask yourself how you imagine your life would be different/better if you had X. The answer to that question will most likely represent your *real need*, the thing you should not be flexible about or allow others to question. Once you know your real need, you should take time to brainstorm — alone or with others — all the possible ways you could meet that need on a reasonable timetable (the how and the when). This approach to help-seeking aids you in overcoming anxiety by making you feel capable of meeting your needs to feel healthy, fulfilled, and supported by others.

SETTING BOUNDARIES

Boundary-setting is the final skill that many anxious people need to develop to experience the full, healing power of relationships. My book *God Help Me, These People are Driving Me Nuts* is dedicated to the topic of setting charitable boundaries. For our purposes, boundary-setting comes in two flavors: saying no and setting limits.

SAYING "NO"

It is not unusual for anxious people to be bad at saying "no." Anxiously attached people are especially bad at this because they fear that saying "no" even to unreasonable, inappropriate, or possibly immoral demands will cause other people to disapprove of and abandon them. Once you have determined that you should say "no" to something, you can use the emotional seesaw exercise to work through the desolations that might prevent you from moving forward, but how do you know whether to say "no" in the first place?

The key is a good sense of the time and energy it takes to attend proficiently to the work and responsibilities over which God has given you primary stewardship. People who are good at managing stress and anxiety know how much time and energy they need to fulfill their primary work or roles and maintain their primary relationships. They reserve the appropriate amount of time and energy for these responsibilities and relationships first because they know no one else can fulfill these responsibilities as well as they can. These are the responsibilities they are most accountable to God for. They are thoughtful about the time they need to give their employer for a just day's work; the time they need to give their home for it to run well; the time they need to give their spouse and children for opportunities to work, talk, play and pray together; and the time they need give themselves to maintain their own personal spiritual life, health, and sanity.

Having established the appropriate amount of time and energy for their primary work and relationships, they decide how to distribute whatever is left among the multitude of opportunities to learn, serve, and grow offered in the modern world.

The degree to which a person is anxious tends to be the degree to which she does exactly the opposite of this strategy. The anxious person will say "yes" to whatever is in front of her, and then work all night and on weekends getting her work done, ignoring any personal needs for spiritual connection, health, or sanity. She hopes that her spouse and children will just understand that "I am busy right now" and "We'll get some time together … tomorrow, or this weekend, or, you know, eventually."

Nobody balances everything perfectly. We all struggle to some degree with maintaining our priorities. But less anxious people understand first things first: the work, roles, and relationships (including with God and themselves) for which they are primarily responsible. They use this criteria for evaluating when to say "no," "not now," or give what I call a "qualified 'yes'" to anything that attempts to threaten their ability to properly attend to their primary work and relationships. It's worth spending a moment on the qualified yes technique.

This technique allows you to be as generous as possible without jeopardizing your primary obligations. The qualified yes technique allows you to refuse a request, but at the same time let the other person know that you might be available to help if the how and when are flexible. For instance, if someone says, "Can you serve on the parents' committee at school?" and you simply don't have the time right now, but you wouldn't mind serving in the future, the qualified yes technique would have you respond, "I would be happy to next semester, but this semester is too busy." If someone asked you to help them with a project Saturday morning, but that time wasn't convenient for you, the qualified yes technique would have you respond, "I would love to help, but Saturday is bad for me. How about next Tuesday?"

Rather than seeing a request as a simple yes or no, the qualified yes technique allows you to acknowledge the value of what the person is asking, but negotiate the how and the when. Sometimes, a person will simply say, "No, I really needed to get it done Saturday." In which case, they actually end up saying "no" to you, which is a much more comfortable position to be in.

There are, of course, times when you simply must say "no." If someone is asking you to do something that is immoral, demeaning, or actively prevents you from attending to your primary responsibilities, then you must refuse. But these situations are surprisingly rare. If you struggle with saying "no," you can deal with most requests gracefully using the qualified yes technique. This enables you to be as generous as possible while protecting your priorities.

For Reflection: Think of a time when you feel more or less on top of your work, your family life, and your self-care. These can be separate occasions. How much time does it actually take to maintain these primary responsibilities, if not perfectly, then at least reasonably well? What changes would you need to make to do a better job of prioritizing this amount of time for each of these responsibilities on a daily/weekly basis?

When do you have a hard time saying "no"? How would you use the suggestions above to do a better job of maintaining your priorities?

SETTING LIMITS

Anxious people often struggle to set limits. Setting limits refers to your ability to insulate yourself from other people's offensive behavior — whether those offenses are intended or accidental. Again, if you have an anxious attachment style you may struggle with this, especially as you may tend to believe — on a deep, unconscious level — that it is somehow your fault that you are being treated poorly.

No one *ever* has the right to treat you disrespectfully, even if you have done something hurtful or offensive first. The more you believe this truth, the less anxious your relationships will make you.

"But … " you might say, "if I do something wrong, doesn't someone have a right to yell at me (or pout, or say mean things, etc.)?" The answer is no. Now, obviously, if you have behaved offensively in some way, other people do have a right to call you on it, and you need to own it, apologize, and make amends. But even when we behave poorly, we are still children of God who deserve to be corrected in a spirit of love and respect. As *Theology of the Body* reminds us, "the only logical response to another person is love." My behavior is only righteous, godly, and defensible if, and only if, I am working for your good. Venting my spleen is not working for your good. Pouting, raging, tantrumming, blaming, name-calling, and emotionally manipulating you is not working for your good. Even if you have offended me, I may not, under any circumstances, treat you disrespectfully. I can certainly call your attention to the offense, and I can even impose a consequence if I believe doing so is genuinely working for your good and the overall good of our relationship. But I may not rage at you, call you names, pout, or be emotionally manipulative in any way. If I choose to respond to an offense you committed against me in any of these ways, I am in error. Such a response speaks only to my lack of self-control and has no bearing on you whatsoever.

This leads to the second rule of thumb that less anxious people practice in relationships: "Respect is the price of admission." In other words, you should be willing to listen to anything anyone has to say to you — even the hard things — as long as they approach you respectfully. But if they are not respectful, then no matter how legitimate their points may be underneath all the anger, abuse, and manipulation, you should neither listen nor respond. Instead, you should set a limit.

I discuss limit-setting at length in my book *God Help Me, These People Are Driving Me Nuts: Making Peace with Difficult People.* I recommend checking that out if you need more help setting charitable boundaries. There are, however, three simple limit-setting steps I can introduce here.

1. Clarify
2. Empathize and Redirect
3. Impose a Consequence

1. Clarify

Most people do not consciously and intentionally behave in ways they think are disrespectful. Most of the time when people are offensive, they are reacting out of pain. They genuinely aren't aware of how they are coming across. Think about it. How often do you actually go out of your way to be offensive to someone?

Clarification allows us to hold up a mirror to someone's offensive behavior so that they can (a) reflect on how they are coming across and (b) choose whether they want to continue down that particular path. If someone uses an offensive tone, says something hurtful, or behaves in a hurtful way, the most charitable limit to set is to give the other person a chance to clarify. For instance:

"I'm sure you don't mean anything by it, but that was really hurtful. Is that really what you mean to say?"

"There's just something about the way you said that that seemed kind of attacking. Could you say that again so I can get what you're really trying to tell me?"

"I'm sure I'm reading you wrong, but you're coming off a little hostile. Would you mind saying it a different way so I can really hear you?"

In each of these examples, you are refusing to address the content of what the offensive person is saying. You are not defending yourself or arguing. You are simply holding up a mirror and asking if the other person really intends to come off the way you are taking them. This is the simplest limit to set, but it is tremendously effective in most situations with most basically healthy people.

For Reflection: *Give an example of a situation where you feel someone you care about is speaking or acting in an offensive way. How might you use clarifying to hold up a mirror to this person's behavior and enable them to reflect on more appropriate ways to behave?*

2. Empathize and Redirect

Sometimes the other person's emotional temperature is so high a simple clarification doesn't ensure they speak to you with respect, and it might even cause their behavior to escalate. Again, this is not your fault. It is a reflection on their poor self-control. Nevertheless, you can still use limits to move the conversation toward a more respectful path. You can empathize with their pain, anger, etc., but redirect toward solutions. For instance, imagine you attempt to clarify someone's behavior and they say, "Yes! That's exactly what I meant! I can't believe what an idiot you are!"

In this case, the person isn't paying the price of admission — respect — so you have no obligation to respond to them. You should not defend yourself. You should not argue back. You should not try to convince them they are wrong. If you do, you will be emotionally overpowered and anxiety will result. Instead, you can simply respond in the following way.

"Look, I get that you're upset with me, and I'm really sorry about that. But I'm not clear what the problem is or what, exactly, you'd like to do about it. Help me understand what's going on."

In this example, you are not responding to anything they said. You are simply observing that they are upset (which helps them feel heard without you actually agreeing with them) and pointing them toward clarifying the specific problem and possible solutions.

By redirecting the discussion in this way, you prompt the other person to stop reacting with their emotional brain (limbic system) and start engaging with their thinking brain (cortex). This allows the person to start giving you useful information to work with instead of allowing them to emotionally vomit all over you and expect you to clean up the mess.

For Reflection: Give an example of a conflict between you and another person in which you believe you could effectively use the Empathize and Redirect technique. What, specifically, would you say to redirect the conversation down a more solutions-focused path? How would this be different from your usual approach?

3. Impose a Consequence

Sometimes even the sincerest attempts to empathize and redirect will fail. Although the best of us can lose it once in a while, this is especially true for people who are habitually verbally abusive. In these times, the person we are speaking with is at an 8 or higher on their emotional temperature scale, and it will be impossible to engage in any productive conversation with them until they get control of themselves. At this point, you will need to impose a consequence. There are many different consequences you can use to get a derailed relationship back on track. The simplest is unilaterally shutting down the conversation. Here's how to do it so that it actually works.

"Look, I can see how upset you are, and I am absolutely willing to discuss this with you, but I want to talk about it in a way that will actually do some good. This isn't it. Why don't we both take some time to pray/think about what the problem is and what we'd like to do about it and then get back together at (insert time here). I think we'll both be in a better place to talk through this then."

It will sometimes happen that the other person is so upset that they refuse to take a break. That's okay. Hold the line. Simply let them say whatever they are saying until they run out of steam and then say, "I understand all that. But like I said, talking about it like this won't work. Let's take some time to pray/think about the problem and what we each want to do about it and then get back together at (insert time here)." Keep repeating this as often as necessary until the other person stops.

Please note, this is different than childishly screaming, "I'm done talking about this with you!" and storming out of the room. When setting this limit, you are reassuring the other person you are actually willing to have the conversation. You are proposing a way forward by asking both of you to think about the problem and possible solutions. Finally, you are proposing an actual time to re-engage the discussion rather than ending the conversation and hoping the whole thing goes away.

Assuming they do finally agree to this limit, make sure that when you re-engage the conversation at the proposed time you discuss the problem and possible solutions, not feelings and whose fault it was. For instance, you might say, "I really appreciate you letting us take a break to think/pray about this. I have some thoughts about all this, but since this is obviously important to you, why don't you start by telling me what you think the problem is and what you'd like to do about it?"

For most people (about 90 percent in my experience), this will be enough to set the conversation on a less anxiety-producing, more solution-focused path. If, by contrast, you find that the person actually escalates at this point, or subsequent attempts to re-engage the discussion cause you to pick the fight up right where you left off, you are probably dealing with a situation that involves verbal abuse, poor self-regulation (on one or both parts), or a lack of effective arguing skills on both of your parts. Regardless, professional assistance may be indicated. Check out the resource appendix for help discovering how you can effectively use other consequences to appropriately address the problems in this relationship and decrease any related anxiety.

For Reflection: *Think of a time when it might be helpful to end a conversation in the manner I described above. What, specifically, would you need to say to set this limit? If you think that these consequences would actually escalate the other person, what will you do to get additional help to manage the anxiety caused by this relationship?*

CONCLUSION

Our relationships play an essential role in our mental health. They are the primary way we attempt to meet our temporal, emotional, and psychological needs. When our relationships are unsupportive or unhealthy, many of our needs go unmet. This causes our brain to detect a threat to our optimal functioning. This perceived threat triggers the fear/threat system in our bodies to motivate us to address the relationship problems that are negatively impacting our wellbeing. If these relationship problems go unaddressed over a long period, we may develop generalized anxiety, health problems, and other stress-related impediments to our well-being. For some people, poor relationships have been a way of life for so long that it never even occurs to them that they can live without anxiety or panic. If anything in this chapter resonates with you, I encourage you to do the necessary work for healthier expectations about your relational health. Don't believe that it will be too hard or that somehow you aren't "meant" to have healthy relationships. God created you for loving communion, not only in the next life, but in this one as well. Have the courage to cooperate with God's grace and begin creating that communion now with the people who share your life.

Healthy relationships are not just a luxury that some people luck into and others don't. Healthy relationships are an essential and integral part of our mental health. Healthy relationships support us as we acquire the resources necessary to meet our needs and function at our best. Relationships that discourage us or impede us in our attempts to meet our needs cause anxiety. If we work to prioritize healthy relationships and overcome the injustices that threaten the loving, affirming, supportive communion in which we were created to live, we are cooperating with God's grace to both build his kingdom on earth and claim our share of the peace that is our inheritance as members of the Body of Christ.

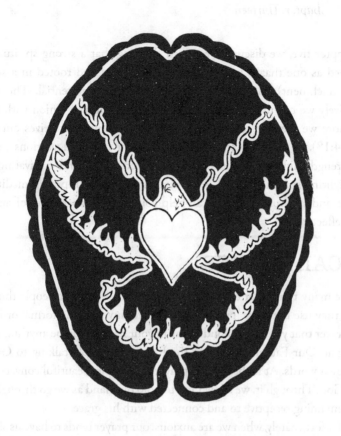

CHAPTER THIRTEEN

Free Us from All Anxiety — Strengthening Your Spiritual Surge Protectors

In chapter five, we discussed research showing that a strong spiritual life (defined as one that is both intrinsically centered and rooted in a secure God-attachment) has powerful anxiety-preventing potential. The more effectively we can use our spiritual resources to cultivate union with God, the more we are able to experience the "perfect love that drives out fear" (1 Jn 4:18). In this chapter, we'll build on some of the suggestions I made for strengthening your spiritual surge protectors — and cultivating this fear-fighting spiritual union — by exploring how vocal prayer, meditative prayer, and spiritual gratitude can help you process experiences of anxiety more effectively.

VOCAL PRAYER

Of the many types that exist, vocal prayer is the one most people think of when they use the word "prayer." Vocal prayer involves any formal or informal prayer that you speak aloud or say in your head. It can be anything from saying an Our Father, to praying the Rosary, to simply talking to God in your own words. At its best, vocal prayer is a simple, beautiful conversation with God. Through it, we allow God to hold our hand as we go through our day, remaining receptive to and connected with his grace.

Unfortunately, when we are anxious, our prayer tends to have us shouting words at God as we strap ourselves in for another roller coaster ride of a day. A quick, "Please, God, help!" or a speedily muttered, white-knuckled, Rosary-in-the-car-on-the-way-to-work is certainly not for nothing. God appreciates whatever time we give him. But instead of being an antidote to anxiety, such prayers often unintentionally reinforce our anxiety. They do nothing to challenge the fact that we have squarely planted both our feet in the quicksand as we desperately beg, "GodhelpmeGodhelpmeGodhelpme ..." and sink up to our necks in the new stresses of the day.

For it to be a truly effective antidote to anxiety, we must take the more reflective approach to prayer I mentioned back chapter two. First, we must approach prayer not with the intention of shouting a quick word at God as we run out the door, but with the intention of stepping out of the chaos. Yes, everything is coming at us at a million miles an hour and we feel like we can't handle it. But, for the Christian, the important thing to remember is that since we genuinely can't handle it all, we should stop trying. Instead, we need to step out of the moment, re-center ourselves in God's grace, and then re-engage the moment holding God's hand. We can do all things through Christ who strengthens us (cf. Phil 4:13). Properly engaged, prayer is the conscious, humble acknowledgement that we desperately need God's help in every moment of our day.

This conscious decision is what Saint John Paul II's *Theology of the Body* refers to as "receptivity." When we actively cultivate a state of receptivity, we are *loving* and *responsible*. This means that, guided by God's hand in a state of receptivity, we are able to respond to every situation in a manner that works for our good and the good of others. Receptivity allows us to choose responses that lead to a more meaningful, intimate, and virtuous life. Recall, from our discussion earlier, that the more we actively, consciously pursue these qualities, the less anxious we will be.

The opposite of receptivity is reactivity. When we are in a state of reactivity, we simply act without thinking of our, or anyone else's, greater good. When we are reactive, we feel powerless and isolated. We give in to self-pity and self-indulgence as we try to "take care of everything ourselves" and fail miserably in the process. Reactivity separates us from grace. It is not sinful, *per se*, but it is — to use an old phrase — a near occasion of sin. Reactivity puts us in a vulnerable position where we can be easily led by the Enemy to do anything to make ourselves feel better now, without any regard for the impact of those choices on our lives, relationships, and wellbeing.

On the face of it, it might seem like you would need to spend hours alone in God's presence to cultivate this spirit of receptivity. Granted, quiet time with God can only help, but the good news is that you don't need to become a hermit. Just like you can take breaks on the fly, you can cultivate receptivity on the fly as well using the following steps.

1. **Slow down.** Slow down your speech. Slow down your actions. Not dramatically, just take an extra beat. Engage your parasympathetic nervous system. Tap your mental brake by intentionally acting and speaking just a little slower than feels natural. Remember

what Elijah discovered in 1 Kings 19:13. God wasn't in the earthquake or the storm. He was in the gentle breeze. We can't effectively communicate with God when we're moving at 100 miles an hour.

2. Lean into love. Before you start praying in earnest, take a few seconds, if not a minute or so, to immerse yourself in God's love. If possible, close your eyes. Say "Jesus, I love you. Help me to feel your love." Repeat this a few times as you breathe deeply. Call to mind the times in your life when you have felt God's love. Allow yourself to re-experience that love now, in this moment. Remember, "Perfect love drives out fear" (1 Jn 4:18). Any prayer is more efficacious if you begin by anchoring yourself in God's love. This is doubly true of any prayer that intends to combat anxiety.

3. Say it out loud. It might seem strange, but when you are struggling with anxiety, it can be much more effective to pray out loud than in your head. If your circumstances permit, talk to God as if he was another person in the room, because he is. Praying out loud helps you to stay focused on your words. Your mind is less likely to wander, especially when you are feeling anxious. Likewise, hearing yourself pray out loud is a great way to begin listening to God. The Holy Spirit often uses our own words to bring certain thoughts or images to mind that he would like us to attend to. Be sensitive to the thoughts, memories, or impulses that come to mind when you hear yourself praying aloud. Assuming that these thoughts, impulses, or memories are leading you to respond in more meaningful, intimate, or virtuous ways to the circumstances of your life, trust that God is reaching out to you and reflect on the significance of these messages.

If you feel at all strange about talking to God out loud, don't. The good news is, with the advent of Bluetooth, no one thinks it's odd to see someone talking out loud to themselves anymore. You can use this cultural dynamic to great spiritual advantage.

4. Pray. Honestly and Thoughtfully. Now, begin to speak to God. Don't sugarcoat anything. Tell him how you really feel. Be honest about your concerns, your frustrations, your fears. Even if you are upset with him, tell him. Be honest and thoughtful in your prayers. Don't just say words at God. Talk to him as if he was an actual person who loves you most and knows you best — because he is! Yes, he is the King of the Universe, but he bids us call him "friend" (Jn 15:15). Talk to your friend. Let him know what is happening in your heart, no matter how scary or ugly it is.

If you prefer to use more formal prayers, that's wonderful, too. The Rosary is a particularly powerful form of meditative prayer that can help you focus on God's love and providence. Just make sure you really bring your heart to it. Reflect on the words as you pray them. Connect those words to what is going on in your life right now. Communicate your needs, hopes, and concerns to God through these beautiful traditional prayers.

5. Listen. Most of us know that prayer is a conversation with God, but most of us treat it as a monologue, not because we don't want to hear God but because we haven't been taught to listen. We will address this in the next section on meditative prayer. For now, it's enough to know that God is always speaking to us. He is never silent. Sometimes we do not know how to listen to him. Sometimes, he speaks in a language that seems foreign to us at first. Sometimes, we don't hear him because his voice comes to us from unexpected directions. But never doubt that he is speaking to you. His voice is peace. His words bring healing to our anxious hearts. Over the next few pages, we'll look more at how to listen, but right now, know that God is speaking to you all day long. Take your cue from what God says in Isaiah 55:3, "Pay attention and come to me; listen, that you may have life."

MEDITATIVE PRAYER

For many people, meditative prayer sounds very mystical and beyond them. In reality, meditative prayer is about learning to listen to God's voice. In meditative prayer, you choose something to focus on. It could be anything. A memory. An experience (past or present). A relationship. A verse of Scripture. Even your body. Choose something that seems — for whatever reason — meaningful to you. Assume that the tug you are feeling to that thing is the Lord gently saying, "Come here. I want to tell you something." Respond to that gentle pull, that sense of significance, and listen. Say, "Lord, speak to me. What are you saying to me through this?"

Anxiety makes us feel alone, powerless, and hopeless. Meditative prayer empowers us in the fight against anxiety by helping us realize that we are never alone, that God is always leading us, and that we can hope in God's plan if not our own power. Imagine that you are a child playing baseball. Feel the weight of the game resting on your shoulders. Now, imagine you hear your coach speaking behind you, reminding you of all the things you have practiced, talking you through the swing. That's what meditative prayer does. It gets you out of your head. It helps you tune in to God coaching you through each moment, reminding you of who you are, of all the things he has already led you through. The more you learn to hear and trust God's voice speaking to you, the more you can resist the pull of anxiety. God is always communicating his love to you, and his love drives out fear.

The simplest way to learn meditative prayer is to practice "active contemplation." Active contemplation has a long history in our Christian tradition. Saint Ignatius recommended it. Saint Thomas Aquinas wrote about it. In fact, most religious orders who are not cloistered (that is, who are engaged in active ministry in the world) view it as a major pillar of their spirituality.

Active contemplation is the ability to step outside of your own feelings about a particular experience and reflect on that same experience from God's point of view. The more you practice active contemplation, the more you can learn to feel that God is leading you, guiding you, and consoling you even in the middle of the most stressful events of your day.

This isn't to say that active contemplation will allow you to float above all the anxiety and swim in a sea of peace at all times. Rather, it will allow you to — as Saint Augustine put it — feel the "press of troubles" without becoming "oppressed." The press of troubles is the stress we feel when life's pressures are mounting up. Oppression is what happens when the press of troubles separates us from God's grace and we begin to feel powerless, isolated, prone to self-pity, and tempted to self-indulgence. Active contemplation enables us to face the press of troubles in a productive way that keeps us connected to both God and others and allows us to experience each moment as a learning experience. In this way, we are able to greet even the hard times with a spirit of hope and confidence that God is with us and (as Julian of Norwich put it) "all shall be well and all manner of things shall be well."

Perhaps the best way to learn active contemplation is to take about five minutes, four times a day, to pray about: (1) what is happening to you; (2) how your body feels; (3) what feelings, thoughts, and memories you are experiencing; and (4) what is the state of your relationships. If you can't find a better time, you can even do this at meal times or while you are going to the bathroom. Don't make a production out of it. Just make it happen however you can. Use the following guide to help you learn to listen to God leading you and guiding you through the anxiety and into a greater place of peace.

1. **What is going on?** In this first five-minute period, reflect on how your day is going. What do you feel good about? What do you feel worried about? What is happening? What things are going to happen as the day moves forward? Keep in mind that God wants you to face all of these things in a spirit of meaningfulness, intimacy, and virtue. Say to God, "Speak to me, Lord. I am listening. Tell me what you want me to know about my day. How do you want me to respond to everything that is happening and will happen today?" Now, prayerfully reflect on your day from God's point of view. What might God be saying to you that would enable you to respond to this day in a more meaningful, intimate, and virtuous manner? What would God want you to remember so that you can resist the temptations to powerlessness, isolation, self-pity, and self-indulgence? Let his love and care wash over you. Listen to his

counsel as he gently guides you in the silence of your heart.

You may not experience any great, earth-shaking movements of the spirit. You probably will not be bowled off your feet. But the more you do this, the more you will experience stronger, gut-level senses that nudge you toward more graceful, meaningful, intimate, and virtuous responses to your day. These "senses" that lead to such responses are the voice of God. Learn to hear them, trust them, and respond to them.

2. How does my body feel? Saint John Paul II's *Theology of the Body* reminds us that God is speaking to us even through the design of our body. Remember, God created your body to function at its best. As Saint Irenaeus reminds us, "The glory of God is man, fully alive!" What is God saying to you through your body? Are you tired or rested? Sore or pain-free? Tense or relaxed? Hungry or full? Cold or hot? Fit or lethargic? In this second five-minute period, consider what God might be saying to you, through your body, about how he wants you to care for yourself. Is he asking you to exercise? Slow down? Get some rest? Eat a little healthier? Stretch? How does God want you to love the body he has given you, to care for your body so that it can do all the wonderful things he created it to do with confidence, strength, and joy?

3. Feelings, thoughts, and memories. In this third five-minute period, bring your mental life to God. What feelings are you having about your day? What memories (recent or childhood) are being triggered by the events of this day? What thoughts or conversations are going through your head? Imagine God teaching you to respond to these feelings, memories, and thoughts in a more meaningful, intimate, or virtuous way. What would he say to you? Does God want you to be defined by these feelings, thoughts, or memories? Why or why not? Are there other, more helpful feelings, thoughts, or memories God would like you to keep in mind as you go about the rest of your day? How would keeping these things in mind help you be more of the whole, healed, godly, grace-filled person God wants you to be? How could you hold onto them?

4. Your relationships. In this last five-minute period, prayerfully consider your relationships with the people in your life. How did the people you encountered today make you feel? What is God saying to you about these people that would allow you to respond to them in a more meaningful, intimate, or virtuous way? Are the people in your life presenting you with an opportunity to become a more whole, healed, godly, grace-filled person? How? Do you feel as close to the people in your life as you need to feel to be at your best? How might God counsel you to close these gaps? What small things could you do today to draw closer to the people he has placed in your life to love and support you? How has he shown you his love through the people you have encountered today?

Of course, you can practice active contemplation outside of these five-minute periods. In fact, the entire point of carving out these periods for more thoughtful reflection of your circumstances, body, mind, and relationships is so that you can become more aware that God is speaking to you through everything you experience all day long. Prayer should not end when you say "Amen." The word "Amen" is from the Hebrew, meaning, "Let it be done!" When you say "Amen" you are, in effect, promising to listen to and observe how God is moving throughout every moment of every day, looking for opportunities to seek and cooperate with his will. The more we practice this, the more anxiety-proof we become as we become aware of God moving in, through, and around us. We feel less alone and more aware of his presence leading us and guiding us through the storms of life. When God is for us, who can be against us (cf. Rom 8:31)?

LECTIO DIVINA

A second ancient type of meditative prayer that has great anxiety-fighting power is *lectio divina*, or "divine reading." This is the process of reflecting on a piece of Scripture (either one verse or several) and prayerfully considering how God is speaking to you through it. As with all forms of meditative prayer, we operate under the assumption that there are no coincidences. If your heart is drawn to something, it isn't because you tripped over it, stumbled across it, or "lucked" into it. It is because that Holy Spirit said to your heart, "Look at this. I want to tell you something."

As we noted in the first chapter of this book, there are several hundred Scripture passages that speak to God's desire to set us free from anxiety and increase our peace, trust, and confidence in him. The more we reflect on these Scripture passages, the more God's Word speaks to our hearts, enabling us to combat the spirits of fear that plague us and strive to push us off the path of grace.

There are five steps of *lectio divina* that can be easily adapted to allow us to create a spiritual action plan against fear, worry, and anxiety. To learn to use these steps in your battle against anxiety, choose one of the verses in the first chapter of this book that speaks to you — or another verse that has personal meaning — and consider the following.

> **Step One: Read (*Lectio*).** Read the verse of Scripture prayerfully. What is the obvious message of this text? What should anyone be able to take from this passage regardless of the circumstances of their life? Write your thoughts in your notebook.

> **Step Two: Meditate (*Meditatio*).** Consider this passage in light of your life and present circumstances. What is God saying to you, personally, through this Scripture? What specific counsel is he giving you through this passage? Write down your thoughts.

> **Step Three: Pray (*Oratio*).** What is your response to God's message to you? Do you want to follow his counsel? Are you grateful? Will it be hard? What graces do you need to faithfully respond to his message? Write down your thoughts.

> **Step Four: Contemplation (*Contemplatio*).** Rest in God's pres-

ence. How is God asking you to renew/reform your mind, your heart, or your life in response to this passage? What is he calling you to do? Write down your thoughts.

Step Five: Action (*Actio*). As you step away from your time of reflection, how will you use this encounter with God's Word to make a more meaningful, intimate, virtuous response to the people and circumstances of your life that are the source of your anxiety? What concrete steps will you take to come against the spirits of oppression and fear you often encounter in your day? Write down your thoughts.

Each time you pray using *lectio divina*, you can return again and again to the same Scripture or you can focus on a different verse the Lord has called your attention to. The point is to begin seeing Scripture as an invitation to a deeper, transforming relationship with the Lord. Let him speak to you through his Word. Open your heart and receive the grace and instruction you need to enter more deeply into the "peace beyond all understanding."

Gratitude Exercises

Multiple studies have shown the power of gratitude for fighting anxiety. A 2016 study in the journal *Self and Identity* found that people who practiced intentional gratitude-based exercises (like gratitude journaling and writing thank-you letters) reported significantly less anxiety and a greater ability to bounce back from stress and anxiety-producing events. This is just one of dozens of research projects that have shown the power of gratitude.

There are two simple gratitude-based exercises that can be tremendously helpful. The first is keeping a blessings journal. Each day, write down all the small but significant blessings you encountered that day. Don't force it, but try to avoid generic, repetitive entries. For instance, instead of just writing "I'm grateful for my family" every day, write something specific about your interactions with your family for which you are grateful. Did someone make you laugh? Did he offer you meaningful help? Did she say something that helped you feel especially loved?

Writing it down is important. First, writing forces you to focus on the task. Second, it allows you to review your lists from day to day. One study found that doing this simple exercise increased participants' happiness set-point (the basic level of average happiness a person experiences from day-to-day) by 25 percent. After each entry, take a moment to say, aloud if possible "Thank you, Lord for showing me that you love me by …" then re-read the entry. Stop to reflect on all the little ways God is showing you his love and care throughout the day. Remind yourself in prayer that you are not alone.

A second gratitude-building exercise is a sacrifice of praise. I first referenced this idea in chapter two. You make a sacrifice of praise anytime you feel stressed, anxious, or overwrought — you know, anytime you feel like doing anything but praising God. Take out your blessings journal and write out a list of times in your life when you felt like you were in over your head but God carried you through. For instance, "I remember when I was afraid I was going to lose my job but God helped me find an even better position." "I remember when I was afraid my friend was angry with me, but God helped us work things out."

Take fifteen minutes to write down as many examples of times God delivered you from hardship as you can think of. Then re-read the list, each time saying, aloud if possible: "I praise you, Lord, because you …" and at the end of the entry, say, "And so, Jesus, I trust in you." For instance, "I praise you, Lord, because I remember when I was afraid of losing my job and you found me an even better one. And so, Jesus, I trust in you."

This simple exercise helps re-orient your mind and spirit to all the times you were tempted to doubt God's providence but experienced his faithfulness despite your fears. Taking just fifteen minutes to write out a sacrifice of praise helps you remember that if God has been faithful to you so many times before, he will not let you down now.

Some people who are anxious have a tendency to believe that there is an invisible tally sheet in heaven. They think, "Sure, God saved me those 10, 100, 1000 times, but *this* is going to be the time that he drops me." Remember Deuteronomy 31:6, "Be strong and steadfast; have no fear or dread … for it is the LORD, your God, who marches with you; he will never fail you or forsake you." Remember that even though we struggle to be faithful, God, the Good Shepherd, is always faithful, ready to seek the lost and carry us back in his arms.

Retreat!

Of course, sometimes, it is essential to get some alone time with God. Taking regular time to sit in his presence in the Blessed Sacrament, go on a retreat, or engage in some other extended period of spiritual reflection or renewal can be tremendously important. Although the other ideas in this chapter may help you in your day-to-day fight against stress and anxiety, there is nothing like taking a weekend or more away from the pressures of daily life to sit in God's presence and allow him to minister to your heart in a deeper way. If it has been a while since you have made a retreat, or you have never been, ask your pastor or contact the adult faith formation office of your diocese to learn about local opportunities to spend some one-on-one time with the Lord.

Spiritual retreats are an essential part of regular spiritual maintenance, especially if your faith has been more extrinsic (i.e., dutiful, habitual) or you have an insecure God-attachment. Make a point of taking at least one weekend per year to plan a getaway with God and reflect on the blessings of the past year and the ways you might more effectively cooperate with his grace in the coming months.

God longs to heal you, to allow you to experience his providence and peace. Invest a little time in the spiritual exercises described in this chapter, and others like them, and allow God to minister to your heart in new and surprising ways. Take a little time with him each day and let him grant you a taste of the peace the world cannot give.

CHAPTER FOURTEEN

The Way of Peace

"Peace I leave with you; my peace I give to you. Not as the world gives do I give it to you. Do not let your hearts be troubled or afraid." (John 14:27)

Throughout this book, I have challenged and encouraged you to see that, as common as the experience of anxiety is, it is not God's plan for our lives. While it may not be possible to completely rid ourselves of all stress, worry, and anxiety in this lifetime, anxiety does not represent God's will for us. In fact, he desires for us to become the whole, healed, godly, grace-filled versions of ourselves — the saintly versions — so consumed by his perfect love that we have room in our hearts only for the peace he leaves with us.

That said, the way of peace is a lifelong journey. We long to be delivered, in one fell swoop, from all the things that cause us to be stressed, worried, and anxious. But the most important thing is not for that deliverance to happen immediately, but rather for us to be confident that by doing whatever we can today — no matter how small — God will give us the peace we are seeking.

I take great comfort in the story of Jesus feeding the multitude. We may often feel that the task before us is too great, that our resources are limited to the equivalent of five loaves and two fish. Sure that nothing I do will be sufficient to meet my needs or overcome my problems, I feel God moving in my heart, asking me to give him what little I have and trust that, somehow, through his grace, it will be more than enough.

I want to thank you for allowing me to accompany you on this part of your journey. I've attempted to share many different ideas to help you in your struggle against anxiety. I sincerely hope that you will find these strategies useful as you continue forward. I am sure there will be many days where you feel like nothing you have read here, and no other resources you may have gathered on your own, could possibly be sufficient to bridge the gap between the anxiety you feel in your heart and the peace you long for. In those times, I ask that you remember the story of the loaves and fishes and trust that the tiny effort you make in this moment, united with God's grace, will be enough to achieve the peace you seek. Continue taking one moment, one small step at a time, making one tiny change, and with God's grace, he will see that it is enough.

In Matthew 17:20, Jesus makes a remarkable promise: "I say to you, if you have faith the size of a mustard seed, you will say to this mountain, 'Move from here to there,' and it will move. Nothing will be impossible for you." Sometimes, anxiety can make us feel like a mountain has been dropped on our chest. Pinned under the incredible weight of everything we have to contend with in our lives, we may feel like we can barely move. How can we ever hope to escape? But even in these times, we can move a millimeter, and that is all God asks. He will do the rest. Why a millimeter? That is the actual size of a mustard seed. In those times when you are sure there is nothing you can do, nothing that will help, no one who could possibly understand, much less deliver you from the press of troubles that is keeping you up at night and distracting you throughout the day, ask yourself to move a millimeter toward meeting the physical, emotional, relational, or spiritual needs that stand between you and the peace you seek. A millimeter. That's all, and it's enough. Find the faith to make even this tiny move toward greater meaningfulness, intimacy, and virtue, and God promises you that he will do everything necessary to take that mountain of anxiety off your chest and cast it into the sea of his mercy, love, and peace.

Of course, there are times when it can seem like moving even that millimeter is too much. In those times, it can be helpful to have someone next to you, a Simon of Cyrene who can help you carry your cross. If you find yourself in this position, I hope you will not hesitate to reach out for help from those people God has placed in your path to offer assistance along the way. In those times when local, faithful resources seem thin, the Pastoral Solutions Institute stands ready to assist you in seeking faith-filled solutions to all the anxiety-producing challenges you face in your life and relationships. To discover more about our Catholic tele-counseling and tele-spiritual direction services, as well as all the other resources we have available to help you on your journey, I hope you visit us at CatholicCounselors.com.

I am grateful for the time we have spent together. I pray that God will bless you abundantly as you walk forward in courage and grace, confident in the knowledge that Our Lord desires for you to receive the peace that is his gift to you, a peace that is not of this world. Do not let your heart be troubled. Do not be afraid.

Resources

To locate faithful, professional counseling resources in your area, contact the Pastoral Solutions Institute for assistance at CatholicCounselors.com or 740-266-6461.

Books

Dr. Tim Clinton, *God Attachment: Why You Believe, Act, and Feel the Way You Do about God* (Howard Books)

Dr. Gregory K. Popcak, *God Help Me, These People Are Driving Me Nuts: Making Peace with Difficult People* (The Crossroad Publishing Company)

Works Cited

Allport, Gordon W., and J. Michael Ross. "Personal religious orientation and prejudice." *Journal of Personality and Social Psychology* 5, no. 4 (April 1967): 432–443, https://dx.doi.org/10.1037/h0021212.

Anxiety and Depression Association of America. "About ADAA: Facts & Statistics." https://adaa.org/about-adaa/press-room/facts-statistics.

———. "Understand the Facts: Sleep Disorders." https://adaa.org/understanding-anxiety/related-illnesses/sleep-disorders.

von Balthasar, Hans Urs. *The Christian and Anxiety.* San Francisco: Ignatius Press, 2000.

Beck, Richard, and Angie McDonald. "Attachment to God: The

Attachment to God Inventory, Tests of Working Model
Correspondence, and an Exploration of Faith Group Differences."
Journal of Psychology and Theology 32, no. 2 (June 2004): 92–103,
https://doi.org/10.1177/009164710403200202.

Cozolino, Louis. *The Neuroscience of Human Relationships: Attachment and
the Developing Social Brain*, 2nd edition. New York: W. W. Norton
& Company, 2014.

Donovan, Michelle. "Workouts to remember: new research suggests
high-intensity exercise boosts memory." *Daily News*, November
22, 2017, McMaster University, https://dailynews.mcmaster
.ca/article/workouts-to-remember-new-research-suggests-high-
intensity-exercise-boosts-memory/.

Emmons, Robert. *Thanks!: How the New Science of Gratitude Can Make
You Happier*. New York: Houghton Mifflin, 2007.

Gerbarg, Patricia L., Philip R. Muskin, and Richard P. Brown, eds.
Complementary and Integrative Treatments in Psychiatric Practice.
Arlington: American Psychiatric Association Publishing, 2017.

Gibala, Martin, Dr. "High-intensity interval training: Is it really the holy
grail of exercise?" *The Globe and Mail*, February 13, 2014. https://
www.theglobeandmail.com/life/health-and-fitness/health-
advisor/high-intensity-interval-training-is-it-really-the-holy-grail-
of-exercise/article16891839/#dashboard/follows/.

Goodrich, Terry. "Can Writing Your 'To-Do's' Help You to Doze?
Baylor Study Suggests Jotting Down Tasks Can Speed the
Trip to Dreamland." *Baylor Media Communications*, January
11, 2018, Baylor University, https://www.baylor.edu/
mediacommunications/news.php?action=story&story=192388.

Gorgoni, Maurizio, Aurora D'Atri, Giulia Lauri, Paolo Maria Rossini,
Fabio Ferlazzo, and Luigi De Gennaro. "Is Sleep Essential for
Neural Plasticity in Humans, and How Does It Affect Motor and
Cognitive Recovery?" *Neural Plasticity* 2013: 1–13, https://doi
.org/10.1155/2013/103949.

Gottman, John M., and Nan Silver. *The Seven Principles for Making
Marriage Work: A Practical Guide from the Country's Foremost*

Relationship Expert. New York: Harmony Books, 2015.

Hirschkowitz, M. "National Sleep Foundation's sleep time duration recommendations: methodology and results summary." *Sleep Health* 1, no. 1 (March 2015): 40–43, http://dx.doi .org/10.1016/j.sleh.2014.12.010.

Huber, B. Rose. "Four in 10 infants lack strong parental attachments." *Princeton News*, March 27, 2014, Princeton University, https:// www.princeton.edu/news/2014/03/27/four-10-infants-lack-strong-parental-attachments.

John Paul II, Saint. *The Theology of the Body: Human Love in the Divine Plan*. Pauline Books & Media, 1997.

Klika, Brett, and Chris Jordan. "High-Intensity Circuit Training Using Body Weight: Maximum Results with Minimal Investment." *ACSM's Health & Fitness Journal* 17, no. 3 (May 2013): 8–13, http://doi.org/10.1249/FIT.0b013e31828cb1e8.

Kowalska, Faustina, Saint. *Diary — Divine Mercy in My Soul*, Notebook V.

Lewandowski Gary W., Jr., Arthur Aron, Sharon Bassis, and Johnna Kunak. "Losing a self-expanding relationship: Implications for the self-concept." *Personal Relationships* 13, no. 3 (August 2006): 317–331, https://doi.org/10.1111/j.1475-6811.2006.00120.x.

Manninen, Sandra, Lauri Tuominen Robin Dunbar, tomi Karjalainen, Jussi Hirvonen, Eveliina Arponen, Riitta Hari, Iiro P. Jääskeläinen, Mikko Sams, and Lauri Nummenmaa. "Social Laughter Triggers Endogenous Opioid Release in Humans." *Journal of Neuroscience* 37, no. 25 (May 2017): 1–20, https://doi.org/10.1523/JNEUROSCI.0688-16.2017.

Matthews, Gillian A., Edward H. Nieh, and Caitlin M. Vander Weele. "Dorsal Raphe Dopamine Neurons Represent the Experience of Social Isolation." *Cell* 164, no. 4 (Feb 2016): 617–631, https://doi.org/10.1016/j.cell.2015.12.040.

Mayo Clinic. "Depression and anxiety: Exercise eases symptoms." https:// www.mayoclinic.org/diseases-conditions/depression/in-depth/depression-and-exercise/art-20046495.

Naidoo, Uma. "Nutritional strategies to ease anxiety." *Harvard Health*

Publishing, April 13, 2016, Harvard Medical School, https://
www.health.harvard.edu/blog/nutritional-strategies-to-ease-
anxiety-201604139441.

Neufeld, Gordon, and Gabor Maté. *Hold On to Your Kids: Why Parents
Need to Matter More Than Peers*. New York: Ballantine Books,
2014.

Nokia, Miriam S., Sanna Lensu, Juha P. Ahtiainen, Petra P. Johansson,
Lauren G. Koch, Steven L. Britton, and Heikki Kainulainen.
"Physical exercise increases adult hippocampal neurogenesis in
male rats provided it is aerobic and sustained." *The Journal of
Psychology* Vol. 594, No. 7. February 4, 2016. https://physoc
.onlinelibrary.wiley.com/doi/abs/10.1113/JP271552 .

Norwegian University of Science and Technology. "Social anxiety
disorders? Cognitive therapy most effective treatment."
ScienceDaily, December 16, 2016, https://www.sciencedaily.com/
releases/2016/12/161216115526.htm.

Petrocchi, Nicola, and Alessandro Couyoumdjian. "The impact of gratitude
on depression and anxiety: the mediating role of criticizing,
attacking, and reassuring the self." *Self and Identity* 15, no. 2
(October 2015): 191–205, https://doi.org/10.1080/15298868.2
015.1095794.

Podles, Leon J. "Unhappy Fault." *Touchstone: A Journal of Mere Christianity*.
The Fellowship of St. James, http://www.touchstonemag.com/
archives/article.php?id=22-06-012-v.

Schermerhorn, Alice C. "Associations of child emotion recognition with
interparental conflict and shy child temperament traits." *Journal
of Social and Personal Relationships*, March 13, 2018, https://doi
.org/10.1177/0265407518762606.

Gaspard, Terry. "Timing Is Everything When It Comes to Marriage
Counseling." *The Gottman Relationship Blog*, The Gottman
Institute, July 23, 2015. https://www.gottman.com/blog/timing-
is-everything-when-it-comes-to-marriage-counseling/.

Tillich, Paul. *Systematic Theology*, Volume 1. Chicago: University of
Chicago Press, 1973.

Vatican Council II. Pastoral Constitution on the Church in the Modern World (*Gaudium et spes*). http://www.vatican.va/archive/hist_councils/ii_vatican_council/documents/vat-ii_const_19651207_gaudium-et-spes_en.html.

Vitz, Paul and Christina P. Lynch. "Thérèse of Lisieux From the Perspective of Attachment Theory and Separation Anxiety." *The International Journal for the Psychology of Religion* 17, no. 1 (December 2007): 61–80, https://doi.org/10.1080/10508610709336854.

Woelk, H., and S. Schläfke. "A multi-center, double-blind, randomized study of the Lavender oil preparation Silexan in comparison to Lorazepam for generalized anxiety disorder." *Phytomedicine* 17, no. 2 (Feb 2010): 94–99, https://doi.org/10.1016/j.phymed.2009.10.006.

ABOUT THE AUTHOR

Dr. Gregory Popcak is the founder/director of CatholicCounselors.com, a Catholic tele-counseling practice providing faithful solutions to tough marriage, family, and personal problems. A Fellow of the American Association of Pastoral Counselors and a Board Certified Diplomate in Clinical Social Work, Dr. Popcak serves as an Associate Professor of Pastoral Studies and the director of the online Master of Arts in Pastoral Studies program at Holy Apostles College. Together with his wife, Lisa, he hosts More2Life, which airs each weekday at 10 a.m. Eastern/9 a.m. Central on EWTN Radio affiliates across the country and on SiriusXM130.